THE
MASK
OF POWER

LYNN V. ANDREWS

THE
MASK
OF POWER

Discovering Your Sacred Self

HarperSanFrancisco

A Division of HarperCollins*Publishers*

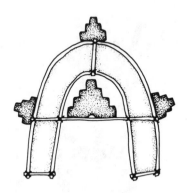

Illustrations by Delia Frees   *Design by Ann Flanagan and Sharon Smith*

FIRST EDITION

Library of Congress Cataloging-in-Publication Data
Andrews, Lynn V.
  The mask of power : discovering your sacred self / Lynn V. Andrews.
— 1st ed.
    P.   cm.
    ISBN 0–06–250012–0
    1. Andrews, Lynn V.   2. Shamanism.   3. Meditations.   I. Title.
  BP610.A54145 1992
  291—dc20   91–58318
                                                              CIP

---

    92 93 94 95 96 HAD   10 9 8 7 6 5 4 3 2 1
    This edition is printed on acid-free paper that meets the American National Standards Institute Z39.48 Standard.

For the Clan of the Whistling Elk and all those who make the
gathering at Joshua Tree possible.

With special acknowledgment to Kathryn Duckworth
for her tireless faith in this workbook.

I would also like to give special acknowledgment to Pat Spear
for her creativity and wonderful energy
during the mask-making process.

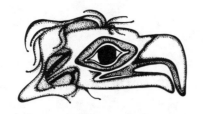

CONTENTS

MASKS OF THE FOUR DIRECTIONS: A PRAYER

Great Spirit,
Powers of the four directions,
My medicine, my allies, my ancestors,
And all those who love me,
Thank you for being with us today.

Great Spirit,
I hold up my shaman face of the south.
In trust and innocence
I give this face to the world.
It is the child within me that sees through this mask
And sees into the world with humbleness and stillness.
Inside I am still the child
With bright eyes, looking out at the world
With hope and joy.

Great Spirit,
May you tend to me on my path.

O great powers of the west,
Powers of the sacred dream,
Death and rebirth, transformation,
See my shaman face,
That part of me that dares to dream,
That dares to move out into the world
Through the intent of my shaman center.

My eyes look through the eyes of this shaman face,
My eyes of my adolescent self,
That part of me that is so full of emotions,
That part of me that needs to understand
The dimensions of death and life
And the never-ending circle of creation.

O great formidable powers of the north,
Home of White Buffalo Woman,
Who brought the sacred pipe to her people,
Powers of the north,
Strength and wisdom, spirit,
I hold up my shaman face.
I am proud.

I look through the eyes of my adult self,
And I see the world with courage and strength.
I stand in my power self,
Holding my shaman face for all the world to see.
And I am not afraid.

Powers of the east,
With your illumination
And your golden sun
That shines so high in the sky,
Help me to understand the other faces of my inner circle.
Help me to bring light
Into those dark corners of my being
So that I may understand even the dark side of myself
And may accept all of my frailties,
As well as my strengths.

Place of illumination,
Place of the sacred clown,
Powers of the east,
Help me to test the existing institutions in my life,
Not with judgment,
But with understanding and knowledge.

It is you, place of illumination,
My shaman face of power,
That helps me to understand what is real and what is true.
Hear my voice
As I speak through my shaman face of the east,
And know that I am real,
And know that I stand in the place of self,
In the center of my sacred wheel.

I have my four shaman faces around me,
And I know that I can wear one or another
As is appropriate in my life.

Great Spirit,
Give me the vision to move into my life with power.

Great Spirit,
Give me the wisdom to know what is right and true.
As I see light in the world,
I reflect that light with the courage of my being.

Great Spirit,
I am yours.
I am like a hollow log
With your energy flowing through me endlessly.
I am yours to do your will,
To live in the light forevermore.
Ho.

PREFACE

The shamanism that I teach comes from the tradition taught by the Sisterhood of the Shields—an extraordinary group of native women who have transmitted their secret wisdom to their daughters and apprentices throughout time. In *Teachings Around the Sacred Wheel,* I defined a shaman as "someone who understands and learns to choreograph the energies of the universe in order to heal the self and others in a sacred way." You and I are the shamans of the twentieth century—no less worthy of the world of sacred healing rituals and of shape shifting than traditional shamans centuries ago, but often much less prepared.

Most of us have moved far away from our instinctual natures, yet deep inside each of us is a longing for the wilderness of the spirit and the power of other worlds. We know we have this magical power, for we get glimpses of it when we travel through inner space in the process of healing ourselves, when we see a baby born, watch a flower bloom, or find the universe contained within an atom. But how do we access this power that we feel all around us, the power that dwells in the mysterious corners of our lives? We have become too accustomed to borrowed knowledge. In school we sit and listen as others tell us about their experiences and dreams. Shamanism, in contrast, arises from our own experiences, and making a shaman face in the form of a mask can help us access our own dreams. Through this process of mask making, you will begin to find within yourself a new vision of reality. Constructing your mask will be like looking into a mirror in which you will be able to see your own unique truth.

As shamans in this age, we are here to heal Mother Earth, but in order to do so, we must first heal ourselves. This is a tall order, since we have walked on this earth perhaps a thousand times before. But there is a reason you chose to be born at this time on this planet, and the reason is clear. You were born in a time when the healing of Mother Earth is imminent, and you would not be reading this here if you did not have certain abilities and gifts that will help in the healing process. Your gift may be simply an instinct that existence is much larger than it seems, or you may have the ability to see auras, to profess the future or the past, or to heal with your hands. Whatever your unique gifts, we will begin to work with them here.

In this book you will be introduced to the gods of fire. By awakening your shaman face, you will experience the power of flame, and you will learn how to arouse the inner fire—a process that allows you to journey through your past lives. The Sisterhood has taught me the importance not only of thoroughly reliving and understanding my past lives but of recognizing and understanding my future lives as well. Through the process described in *The Woman of Wyrrd,* I learned that these lives are held within the flow of the bloodstream. The blood holds both the memory of the past and the vision of the future. This book shows you how to access these memories and visions.

Most of my writing has described my personal journey with my teachers. But along my path of heart, I have received many teachings that are applicable to my readers' lives as well. To make these teachings and acts of power even more accessible to all of you, I began in 1989 to give one group training a year in the high desert of California. For four days and nights, all of the participants commit to a world of mystery and change. Out of that commitment, and the exercises and ceremonies, comes extraordinary growth and the development of mirrors in which we can view ourselves in new ways. Thus, *The Mask of Power* was born at the Clan of the Whistling Elk's third council fire in 1991.

Just as the clan does each year, you will learn here how to make self masks and empower them. Mask making is a tangible way to elicit the heart of your own truth and to unveil false personas. For before you can take your power, you must first identify who you are. This process requires that you look anew at what faces you wear every day and at who the world thinks you are. Through the mask making and meditations in this book, you will learn how to bring to this work a nudity of spirit and how to allow a "losing of face" so that a truer and more powerful image of who you actually are can begin to develop. Only then will your shaman face of power be born.

INTRODUCTION

This training book about shaman masks is the second in a series that began with *Teachings Around the Sacred Wheel*. It comes to you at a special time, just when Agnes Whistling Elk has accomplished something that no one in the Sisterhood has ever done before. As a sign of her great respect and faith in your commitment and ability to manifest your sacred destiny on this earth, she has lent her name to a clan. This new clan is a tributary of the great river of the Sisterhood of the Shields and is named the Clan of the Whistling Elk. Ani, a Nepalese hill woman and member of the Sisterhood, told me several years ago when I was writing *Windhorse Woman* that all things are written by the gods in the great *Book of the Child*. Perhaps there it is written that you, too, are to do this work and become part of the Clan of the Whistling Elk.

To become a clan member or simply to journey further along your path of spiritual evolution, you must first find your shaman face. You must understand the meaning of your shaman face, or mask, and its place on your sacred altar. Your mask and your altar work together, because they are both built from your essential nature. Your shaman mask will become the central focus of your altar.

When I use the word *altar*, every one of you probably has a different impression of what I mean. An altar, to a shaman, really means the "face of the earth." It is a sacred place where one can tune into the powers, the healing energies, the balance of Mother Earth, our primal source of energy. I will teach you in this book how to design an altar and what objects to place on it in order to collect power from you the healer and from the universe.

Altars are exceedingly important at this period in history. Your own unique power as a healer is represented on the altar by your shaman face, your mask of power. Your mask, when initiated through the imagery work described in this book, can become a bridge between the physical world of everyday life and the spiritual world that encompasses the healing dimensions of reality. Ideally, each and every person would have an altar and a shaman mask, as a means of healing ourselves and Mother Earth.

An altar can help you focus your energies into sacred prayer—"prayer" here meaning ritual and ceremony and the healing process. A ceremony, however, is only as powerful as the person performing it; so, too, our prayers are only as powerful as the intent, emotion, and integrity with which we send them to the Great Spirit. As with anything else, we need to learn to pray effectively. How do you call for power? How do you meet your ancestral beings, guardian spirits, and medicine animal, and how do you invite them to join in your ceremony? By learning to do things in ceremonial ways. Using the altar is one of those ways.

An altar can act like a battery, collecting power and energy from the universe. As we learn to be shamans and healers, we learn to use our bodies and spirits as instruments and to coordinate them with our altars. We learn how to project our healing power into the world.

Through focusing meditations, learned skills, and ceremonies, this workbook will enable you to move energetically toward your initiation into the ceremony of the shaman face, or the removal of your "false face," as it is often called by the Sisterhood. You will make your own shaman face, or mask, and learn to use it with your sacred altar. The mask is a spirit bridge. It is a mask of power. It is about theater, art, dance, magic, healing, and the mystery and power of a shaman's soul. To divine this mask, you must know deeply the different aspects of yourself. The meditations and ceremonies in this book will help you identify various aspects of your dark side and your past. You will need to dig up every hidden corner of your soul so that your energy can be refocused toward enlightenment. But I know that you would not be a part of this work were you not already highly committed to it and if you had not already done a great deal of work on yourself.

We operate in the world through an infinite number of personas that represent our beauty or that mask the flaws that we wish to hide. When we inhibit our spontaneity, our instinctual nature, or the flow of the life force, our dark side is manifested. The study of masks allows us to study our souls both within the sacred Dreamtime—the exploration of higher levels of perception—and within our everyday reality, where these personas are at work. You must prepare for your mask to live at the heart of your altar by getting in touch with the personas that you currently wear.

Many of you have studied the power of symbolism. This workbook will help you to draw on what you have learned. Remember that there are many different kinds of masks in the world. As part of your journey, go to the library and read about other traditions and their search for the understanding of the "false face" and marks.

Always remember that we are of the twentieth century. Most of us are not Native American. I am not imparting to you traditional Native American knowledge; instead, this is the knowledge of truth as memorized and taught by the Sisterhood of the Shields throughout the ages. It is, indeed, the ancient and secret power of woman—a wisdom that empowers the female side of men, as well as of women, and that is equally important for men to use and understand. The meditations in this book will help you to balance your male and female shields, or the male and female aspects of yourself.

As always in my work with you, I encourage you to strip away what you think to be true, what you think about yourself, as you would strip away the layers of an onion. Strip away all the old ideologies and feelings so that new light can shine through.

I am sure that you have heard the old adage, when your cup is full—and many of you have very full cups—it needs to be emptied. You may know a great deal, but a lot of that knowing has been borrowed from the experiences of others. It is time to empty your

cup so that you can gain new knowledge and experience. I am here
to help you empty your cup. I want you to let go. I want you to relax
into the safety of this sacred work. Pull it around you like a cocoon,
feel the arms of the Great Mother holding you, and relax into her
arms with faith and trust—faith that the Sisterhood and I know what
we are talking about, and trust that this path can take you to a much
higher level in your own evolution.

The visualizations that we will work with are sacred, not unlike
those taught in Tibet, by native shamans all over the world, by sacred societies and mystery schools in Ephesus and Egypt, and by
others throughout time. The ways in which they are woven together,
the words we use, and the images they evoke are all chosen to pro-
mote a feeling and a tapestry of reality that may be a little new to
you. At times this work will be frightening, at times exhausting, at
times sad and painful, and at times joyful.

I want you to feel all of these moods and emotions, because an
essential element of ceremony is emotion—feelings of power, sadness, excitement, exultation, love. All of these help you to discover
and empower your shaman will. And it is through the will that

creativity is produced in the world. If you use only your mind and not your emotions, you will never be a shaman.

Part of what I will do in this training book is to teach you to see. I want you to see not only what happens around you in your daily life but also the patterns and flow of energy that create these daily events. I want you to begin to sense at least, if not to see, auras and colors around people. As Agnes Whistling Elk has often told me, if a shaman cannot see the weapons and tools, the hidden masks, that a warrior carries, then she or he is not truly a shaman. So it is important that you begin to work on true *seeing*.

These visualizations will exercise "muscles" that you do not know you have. When you begin to work in the meditative state, use your intent and power as best you can. People often tell me that when they first meditate, they drop into an almost trancelike sleep. If you are working with a partner when this happens, be sure to let your partner know, so you may repeat the visualization at another time. You might want to sit up during these meditations so that you do not fall asleep. Or it may be good that you fall asleep; perhaps your conscious mind needs to sleep so that the information can slip directly into the subconscious.

I think it is important for you to understand how this book relates to the four directions on the sacred wheel.

For this workbook we enter the wheel in the south, the direction that represents the child within, trust, innocence, and substance. The actual making of the mask—the physical act of putting it together, having it on your face, drying it, taking it off your face, and of making a mask on another person's face—takes place in the south.

We awaken the mask in the north direction of the wheel, which represents spirit, strength, wisdom, and the adult within. So we move from the south, where we looked toward the north, and then, awakening the mask, we turn in the north and look back to the south. Back in the south we wear the mask and learn to dance with it.

We then move to the west. The west symbolizes the adolescent within us. It also symbolizes emotion, the sacred dream, death and rebirth, transformation. It is with emotion that you must build and use your altar. Build it and use it with the thought of transformation—of healing, of arresting the forces of death, and of moving into a new life. It is in the west that you take your sacred shaman face and place it in the middle of your altar.

Sitting in the west, we look across the sacred wheel at the east. It is in the east that you initiate your shaman face with the sacred fire that glows like the rising sun. It is there, in the direction symbolizing the old wise one within and the mind, that we find our illumination, our wisdom, and our creativity.

At the end of the book, you will have a balanced sacred wheel. You will have many new tools to call upon within your own being. As you work through the pages that follow, please take notes and use the worksheets. If you do not understand some part of the process or if there is any confusion, please take time to discuss it with a partner so you can become clear and move on.

HOW YOU CAN USE THIS BOOK

You can use this book most successfully if you use my taped meditations along with it or if you read the meditations and visualizations beforehand onto tape. It is important to read them exactly as written because the sacred sounds have been woven together precisely for the best energetic effect. Certain vowel and consonant sounds pronounced together release healing energy.

For the actual making of the mask, your experience will be deepened if you work with a partner, because each of you can help and become a mirror for the other.

The masks that we make in this book are self masks that recreate exactly the appearance of our own faces. There are mask-making kits available in art stores, or you can use the instructions in Chapter Three, "How to Make Your Mask," to create your mask from scratch. Both ways are equally effective.

Each visualization works with your spirit, mind, and heart in various aspects of the four directions. As you grow, the visualizations also expand, and new knowledge will be revealed to you as you repeat them throughout your evolutionary process. We only make one mask in this book, but it would be wonderful if you created masks for each of the four directions and for different aspects of the energy beings that live inside you. These energies take the form of power animals, as discussed in *Teachings Around the Sacred Wheel,* or in other personas or guides that you create.

This book also serves as a journal for the journey along your path of heart. Please use it to record every sacred step that you make. It is important to use the worksheets as you proceed so that you have a complete journal of discovery when you finish. This will be of great use to you in the future and will help you to chart your progress and evolution as you create a unique personal history. Perhaps one day you will want to set aside that personal history and step fully into the unknown mysteries of power.

WHAT YOU WILL NEED

Mask:

scissors
towels
headband
petroleum jelly
bowl for water
plaster-impregnated gauze
mirror
acrylic gesso and paintbrushes
smudge stick and sage or cedar
matches

Decorating supplies:

paints, crayons, chalk, markers
different types of brushes
hot glue gun (optional)

Materials that you may want to use as symbols, the four directions, your power animal, and so on may include natural materials, feathers, pinecones, seedpods, sand, shells, crystals, leather thongs, fabric pouches, yarn, ribbon, twine, crochet thread, beads, sequins, mirrors, buttons, and trinkets—items that are symbolically important to you.

In preparation for making your shaman mask, you should study masks at museums, in books, or in shops to get ideas for its decoration. Think about symbols that represent your power animal. If you do not know your power animal, meditate on your allies in the world, such as a favorite animal, the wind, trees, the ocean, crystals, or stones. Use symbols that are meaningful to you. You may also use symbols representing the direction on the sacred wheel in which you work.

A notebook and a tape recorder to record your own voice reading the meditations are also needed. (Tapes are available from me, as well. Please use the address at the back of the book to inquire.)

HOW DOES DISCOVERING YOUR SHAMAN MASK OF POWER FIT INTO YOUR JOURNEY TOWARD SELF-REALIZATION?

If you could perform one act of power that would change your life forever, what do you think it would be?

This is a question I often ask. It brings up a lot of uneasiness and a lot of passion in people because an act of power must be performed from the deepest part of one's being. An act of power is a manifestation of your truth in the world. I talk about acts of power with almost everyone I work with, because we must all go through the four levels, or hoops, of power as we evolve. The first hoop of power is reached during your formative years. While you are in this hoop, you learn to work with your conditioning and the teachings of childhood, and you develop ways of solving your problems. Out of this process you begin to take your power and make your way in life.

Usually, the second hoop of power is reached around middle age. By then you feel as if you are living on a plateau, and above your head is a layer of clouds that you now realize has been there all your life. The clouds have acted as a kind of barrier, keeping you down. You know that there is something up there, above them, but

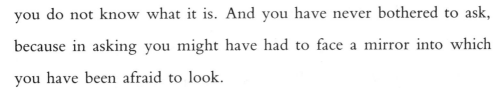

you do not know what it is. And you have never bothered to ask, because in asking you might have had to face a mirror into which you have been afraid to look.

To get through this barrier, you must perform one or two acts of power. An act of power occurs when you take all of your focus, all of your energy, all of your will and intent, and put them into one passionate endeavor. An act of power is like shooting an arrow through the fog. For you, this act may consist of writing a book, composing a piece of music, creating a work of art, or raising a family. Whatever form it takes, it requires that you find your own truth to manifest in the world. The act of power catapults you up out of the first hoop of power and into the second. You move vertically from south to north on the sacred wheel. You take spirit and inspiration from the north and manifest it in the south in the physical realm. Then you reap the benefits, which are mirrored back in the north in wisdom and strength. In other words, a vertical movement of energy is created on your wheel. The act of power causes you to move vertically up through that barrier of flat energy that has been over your head your whole life. This is the movement that creates enlightenment.

You move up above the clouds, into the golden sunlight, into a higher rate of vibration, a new harmonic, where other people who are performing an act of power live. Even though you have been shoulder to shoulder with these people for perhaps many years, you did not realize that their lives were so very different from yours. You have been living below them spiritually, under the overcast, with people similarly situated on the scale of spiritual evolution—all of you basically living in circles of powerlessness.

When you perform an act of power, such as the making of your shaman mask, you move up into the second hoop of power. You can live there perhaps for years, as you begin to manifest your true destiny in this lifetime. But the outcome of your act of power is not just the book you write, the masterpiece of art you create, the magnificent music you compose, the family you raise. The act of power also gathers your strength and energy, creating a burning fire. The fire burns away all of your negativity, all of your blocks and emotional baggage. The very fact that you have performed the act of power rids you of the blocks and problems to which you were giving so much energy and that were preventing you from moving ahead.

An act of power, such as uncovering our false personas, can only be accomplished through an incredible concentration of will, a collection of energy that we call the "shaman will." For many years you may live in the second hoop of power, concentrating your energies and performing acts of power, but eventually you will come to a period in your life when you will know that you have "done it." You will know that you have stretched beyond the boundaries that you thought limited your abilities. You will have stretched into the world of magic, power, strength, and wisdom. You will have built a strong foundation in your being that anchors your life process. This foundation consists of how you take care of your body, how you live with dignity in the world, how you earn a living, how you take care of your family. These serve as mirrors for your self, and they are essential to your growth on the physical plane.

You chose to be born on the physical plane for a reason: to learn lessons you can only learn here, such as how to perform an act of power. Your foundation, your spirit lodge, must be very secure, just as a skyscraper cannot be built on sand. When you move up into the dome of your being, your spirit lodge, and begin to do higher spiritual work and ceremonies, you must be strong—physically, mentally, and emotionally. All of your baggage must be gone or that spirit lodge will come tumbling down.

When you move into the third hoop of power, a different experience happens altogether. The act of power that has taken you through the second hoop generated a tremendous amount of work for you. With the mirrors that you have created through this work, you have managed to drop all your old baggage—pain, difficulties, childhood conditioning. You have traveled closer and closer to the center of your sacred spiral, which is your true and essential self— that home of the magnificent sacred witness, that place within you that is the still point.

Imagine that center as the eye of the storm. All of life circulates around your center in pandemonium, in madness, circulating at different vibrations and rates of speed. And you sit in the center, in ever-increasing stillness, knowing that you have, indeed, accomplished what you have come to accomplish on this earth. You have made your mark. You have changed the world in some way. You have manifested your truth and your being in the world, and now a kind of stillness inhabits you. You begin to watch life like a great wise one. You begin to realize that in this state there is no need, there is no desire. You have already had it all. What people have a hard time understanding is that in order to give something up, you must first own it, you must have it totally. In order to give up your worldly life, your act of power, you must first have performed it and lived it from every direction on the sacred wheel with the totality of your being. Then, when your sacred wheel is complete, the stillness comes, like a great lull. The wind dies down and there is only a gentle breeze. The tumultuousness of your life has been wonderful. Your passion was exquisite, and you are proud of it. But now you sit in the center on your sacred magician's seat, the seat of forgetting and remembering. You live now in the third hoop of power, the next aspect of your sacred life.

It is important to understand that when I say that you reach a place of stillness when you move into the third hoop of power, I do not mean that you are moving into complacency. Often we reach middle life, having accomplished a lot in the material world, and we get lazy. Padding ourselves against any kind of upsetting thoughts, anything that would upset the apple cart, we become rigid in our ideals and our ideas. We have a system that has worked for us, and we are not going to move out of that system for anything, because we have worked very hard to establish it. It has repaid us well. We have reached a level of inertness.

Shamans call this reaching a plateau. Years ago, Agnes Whistling Elk drew me a sand painting. It looked like a dragon or a snake. When I traced the figure up from the bottom to the plateau in the curve of the snake's body, she would say, "You see. This snake represents your life from beginning to end. You go up to the top here, and you feel that you are enlightened. Ah, you have done it. Then you stay there for a short time, and you slide down the back of the snake into a valley. You realize that you know nothing. It is like you are starting all over again. Then you start to climb back up. You reach a pinnacle and you think, 'Ah, now, I've got it—this is it,' only to find it is another plateau, and you slide down into another valley. Realizing you know nothing, you start to climb again and find yourself at another plateau, this time perhaps a little higher but nevertheless a plateau. And then, of course, you realize that you know nothing, and you slide back down into another valley, and so on. Stringing all of these mountains and valleys together is like a snake making its way across the desert floor."

You need to understand this progression through the hoops of power in order to begin to visualize it in your life. Agnes Whistling Elk once told me that when you first contemplate moving from the first hoop of power to the second, it feels as if you are standing on the ground watching a merry-go-round circling in front of you; you want to take a ride, but it will not stop. Finally, you decide that you are just going to leap onto it. The only way to do that, of course, is to back up, take a good run, jump onto the merry-go-round, and hang on for dear life. The second hoop of power moves much faster than the first. It takes an enormously focused, concentrated effort of will to move to that new level, to move your entire being onto the magic carousel.

Not many people reach the third hoop of power in their lifetime; most have not had the guidance, or they are not ready. But I think today more and more people are getting close to it. When you can live in that stillness, in the ecstasy of nondoing, you live with an open heart all of the time. When you can live with an open heart, understanding that behind that open heart is the sacred witness looking out at the world—observing, hearing, and acting but not reacting—*that* is the difference that brings you to the third hoop of power.

We spend most of our lives, even in the second hoop of power, in reaction to the world around us—to our conditioning, to what people do to us, for us, in company with us. In the third hoop of power, *you* begin to be the prime mover. You begin to see the world as a goddess would—simply watching, creating harmony, balance, and a space of tenderness, kindness, and understanding around you. You become the teacher, because now you can see the travail, the pain—both spiritual and physical—that people are living through. It is at this level that you empty your full cup so that something new can be learned. It is at this point that the great masters and the sisterhoods and brotherhoods descend into your life to begin to teach you so that you may move out into the world and teach others.

The fourth hoop of power cannot be described; it can only be experienced. It is a state of purity and love that comes when you realize a total oneness with the Great Spirit.

To move to these higher hoops of power, you need to understand the masks that you wear in everyday life. Most important, your face of power, your shaman mask, must be awakened, for it will play an important role on your sacred shaman's path of choreographing the energies of the universe. Agnes Whistling Elk said to me many years ago that we are all called and we are all chosen, but so very few of us have the courage to follow our dreams and become whole. The process of discovering your "false face" and of creating your shaman face offers one important way to move further along the path to personal power.

CHAPTER 1

MASKS
ON THE
SACRED ALTAR

INTRODUCTION

In the chapter called "Face of the Earth" in *Jaguar Woman,* I speak at length about altars. Remember that your altar is not simply a coffee table with pretty knickknacks on it. It is a place of power, a place where your sacred and precious bundles and objects are collected together. An altar is their home and should be protected and honored just as you protect and honor your own home.

HOW TO BUILD AN ALTAR

The concept of the mask or the discovery of the "false face" is as ancient as time. Masks have been used by shamans throughout the world for as long as there has been recorded history. For the Sisterhood of the Shields, your mask is first your own face, and then, as you enhance it through symbol and ceremony, it becomes your shaman face. When you bring your mask, endowed with aspects of your power animal and of your guides and your individual dreaming, to your first true sacred altar—the altar that has been awakened by the presence of your sister circle, the Sisterhood of the Shields—your mask is no longer just the face of your power animal or your spirit self. It is your own face impregnated with the power of the Great Mother and the Great Spirit.

Your shaman face is the center of your altar. It represents the essence of your being in the physical world and in the spirit world. Your mask is actually the bridge between those two worlds. It is part of the rainbow bridge that you are. What I am is what you all are, a bridge between primal reality and social reality.

When I first went to Agnes Whistling Elk in the far north and became her apprentice, she told me that I was a rainbow bridge between the primal mind and so-called civilized consciousness—that I was to act, in a sense, as a translator for the extraordinary, magical, and powerful world of the wizards, the shamans, and the unknown. I was to bridge that world of power with the world of every day, the world that we call ordinary and physical and present. Agnes also told me that the earth would be saved by the women of the West. She meant that the women of today, the women who understand the energy of Mother Earth—because, indeed, the earth is female—that these women of the West are free to speak. We have a voice in the world. We are not behind the veil. We are the ones who can elevate our spirits and then reach out to guide other women and to guide the men in our lives. The men of the West are also engaged in the process of saving the earth, but first they must be taught about the energy of

Mother Earth by women, by those who understand that energy. I am not saying that men are better than women or that women are better than men. I am not implying anything pejorative. It is simply a fact that the earth is female and that every woman here has always known, on some level, this truth. Unfortunately, we live in a basically patriarchal system that has denied this reality. For this reason, we have had to fight our way back to our own consciousness and awareness as women. We have had to struggle to be able to understand without hate and anger and fear that we are here as the custodians of Mother Earth, that we are here to translate her energy. Were we on a masculine planet, like Mars, the men would need to teach the women.

In other words, we all come here to become enlightened, although this is the one thing that we are most afraid of. Women come here to learn to take their power in the face of great adversity. Men come to learn to deal with their egos. They come here to learn to heal the female side of themselves through the Goddess nature that they find in every woman. All of us are in a period of tremendous flux and transition; thus, it is especially important as healers, as young shamans, to understand that we stand with a foot in each world—one foot in the physical and one foot in the spirit world. Your mask, when you put it on, when you place it on your altar, when you use it in a ceremonial sense, is the bridge between those two worlds. The very act of placing the mask over your face will always be a way for you to enter into the shaman world, the dream-walking world of spirit power.

The home of your spirit mask, your shaman face, is your altar. Now I would like to explain to you how to build an altar. The "face of the earth," as we call the altar, is traditionally rectangular in shape. It can be a table; it can be a stone; it can be an altar cloth stretched out before you. Remember that an altar is like a battery. It holds precious life force and energy. To empower your altar with energy, you must collect certain objects from your life. Basically, the design of the altar is comprised of four triangles whose points face in toward the center, so that the energy of everything placed within those triangles moves toward the center to create a vortex of power. In the center, of course, is your shaman face.

Building an altar requires that we look intimately at both the light and dark sides of ourselves, and Western society discourages

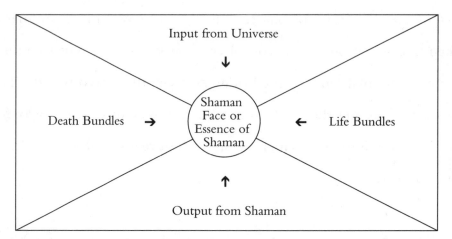

Input from Universe

↓

Death Bundles   →   Shaman Face or Essence of Shaman   ←   Life Bundles

↑

Output from Shaman

most of us from doing this. But as a shaman, this is your task in life: you must go into the wound of your being and discover the pain there. Look at it, experience it, and heal it. Move out on the other side a wounded healer, someone who has moved through the essence of his or her sorrow and found strength. Perhaps you are a shaman precisely because you have come from a home that was either emotionally or physically abusive or because you have lived through a life-denying experience at some point and have come out on the other side with incredible abilities—abilities that allow you not only to survive but also to comprehend a higher reality.

All of your sacred bundles go on the altar, everything that you have deemed sacred in your life, objects that empower you, that are part of your life. Whether it is your doctoral degree or some sand

from your mother's grave, these things empower you. Crystals, your sacred pipe (if you have one), anything that you use in ceremony, anything that has been given to you, that you are proud of—all these go on your altar. I mention sand from a loved one's grave because, to the right and left of your shaman face, you need to balance the positive energy bundles and objects with the negative energy objects, or life bundles with death bundles.

In the triangle above your mask on the altar, you need to bring energy down from the universe through objects that can act as antennae, such as staffs, candles, feathers, and prayer sticks. You must also give energy from yourself as the shaman sitting at the bottom of the altar, sending this energy with crystals and personal power objects through the lower triangle toward the center. All of this is done to endow your altar, the "face of the earth," with power so that when someone in need sits across from you with the altar between you, you can access the levels of energy necessary to heal that person. Those levels of energy are symbolized by the objects on your altar.

Remember that creating your altar is something that you will be working on for a lifetime. Like Rome, an altar cannot be built in a day. An altar grows as you grow—throughout your life.

WORKSHEET

Describe your altar, your prayers for guidance when creating your altar, and how each of the items on your altar balances and empowers each other.

CHAPTER 2

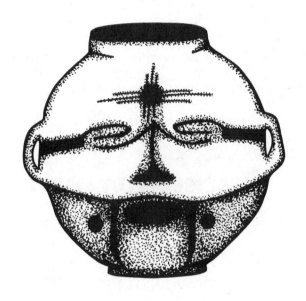

SELF MASK
AT THE LAKE

INTRODUCTION

A lake is often a symbol of the subconscious. In this visualization you will be working with images, people, and feelings buried deep inside your psyche that need to be confronted, talked with, and perhaps readjusted so that you can more easily walk down your path of heart.

EXERCISE/MEDITATION

Close your eyes. Let your mind be still. Allow your breath to drop down into the center of your being, and take this time to relax. As you exhale, say to yourself silently, "I am, I am." As you begin to relax, focus your consciousness on your body. Feel. Sense. Let your feet relax. Your feet ground you with the earth. Feel the bottoms of your feet touching the earth, grounding you. Allow your ankles to relax, and your lower legs. Remember that you can move in the direction of greater comfort and joy at any time if you feel tension. Feel your breath moving through your body. Allow your knees, your thighs, your sexual center to relax completely. Allow your hips and waist to relax. Imagine that even the organs of your midsection are relaxing. Imagine your heart relaxing and your lungs. Let your ribs and chest relax. Allow yourself with each breath to become deeply, deeply relaxed.

Let your shoulders drop. We carry around on our shoulders the weight of the world. Allow your shoulders to relax now and rest easy. Relax your hands, your arms. We can change our lives in simple ways by allowing our hands to relax. Allow your neck to feel deeply, deeply relaxed. Now your body is becoming more centered, more relaxed, more quiet. Relax your facial muscles. Allow your eyes to relax and rest. Allow your scalp to rest. Allow your jaw to go slack. Relax. Relax your whole body. Now place your consciousness again on your breath, as you are deeply and completely relaxed.

The journey we are about to take will be healing and vital for you. In your own way now, in your mind's eye, in your consciousness, I would like you to imagine yourself walking in a forest. Pay attention to each step that you take. Take each step naturally, not with too much consciousness or self-consciousness, but simply be present in each moment, in each step, as you walk along the forest floor. The path is strewn with needles from the forest's large pine trees. The sky can just be seen from the place where you walk among the trees in the forest. The trees blow in the slight wind. You hear birds calling, and you wonder where the birds are. The smell of the pine is rich, and you feel good. As you walk, let yourself know that you are on a journey that will bring healing and peace; you are on a centering journey.

Now you come to a clearing in the forest. Before you stretches a large lake. As you see the lake and walk toward it, you realize that inside each of us is a lake—a lake of beauty, of true depths, of stillness. This lake has been forgotten by most people; they never experience it. Notice the sunlight shining brilliantly in the clearing as you move toward the shimmering water. The sun is truly magnificent at this time of day. Take a moment in silence to walk near the lake, feeling, sensing, and looking for a place where you can make a circle, someplace along the lake and near the forest that feels just right to you. Here, by the water, we will perform a ceremony.

(Pause)

After you have found your special place, take a moment in silence to say a prayer of thanks. Give thanks for your life. Give thanks for your friends and family. Give thanks for this beautiful day. Give

thanks for all the good things you have experienced in life. Give thanks for the difficulties that you have had and how you have learned from them—yes, even for your problems, your worries, your concerns. By blessing them, you release them to the wind, and you call on God, the Great Spirit, the powers of the four directions to help you and guide you. Take time now in the silence to give a prayer of thanks, a prayer for guidance.

(Pause)

Now walk in the forest and find marker stones for the four directions with which to build a sacred circle. First find a stone for the east, then a stone for the south, a stone for the west, and finally a stone for the north. Make your circle large, large enough to sit in, large enough for a number of people to sit in if necessary. Take time in the silence to gather the stones of the four directions.

Now find other stones to complete your circle, to complete the pathway from one of the four directions to the next around the perimeter of the circle. These stones represent the movement of your life, the sacred journey that you are on. Take a few minutes to build your circle, paying attention to each step as you go, gathering each stone with thanks and with love.

After you have completed your circle, journey to your power tree. One of the trees here in this forest is your tree. It is a tree that represents your sacred life in the world. This tree holds power for you and represents your strength, your groundedness, your ability to grow, your ability to rise high and yet remain grounded in the earth. At the base of this tree you will find a beautiful red Indian blanket. You will also find an ancient mask that symbolizes the essence of you. This mask could represent an animal or even a goddess. So go now, and find the mask and the blanket and your sacred tree. Once again, when you find them, say a prayer of thanks. Hug the tree. Sit there for a moment in the silence and listen for any messages that may come.

(Pause)

Now take the blanket, and hold the mask in your hands. Feel the carved edges and note the colors. Then place the mask over your face. It fits perfectly. It was made for you. Peer out of the eyeholes, looking out from the center of your self, from within your mask, from within your shaman place of self. Trust that whatever essence of self you have found is the essence or aspect of yourself that you need right now in the center of your circle; trust that this is your ancient self mask, which has been worn by you in many lifetimes.

Wearing this mask and holding your blanket, walk from your sacred tree back to your circle near the lake. Notice the sun glimmering off the lake. You can see a few birds on the far side of the lake, dipping down to get drinks of water, and you imagine that the lake holds pure water that is good to drink. As you walk up to your circle, prepare to enter it from the east, the place of illumination, the place of sunrise, the place of the new day, the place of creativity. Before you enter the circle, say a prayer. Give thanks from this place of the east.

Enter the circle and move toward the south. From within your self mask, say a prayer to the south for trust and innocence, for guidance in the small details of life. Say a prayer for the ability to pay attention to each step as you go.

Now move to the west, to the place of looking within, the place of dreams and intuition, the place of the woman inside each of us, the place of quiet and introspection, and take time in the silence to say a prayer of thanks.

Move to the north, and here say a prayer for wisdom. Say a prayer that you will be able to give away what you have learned. Say a prayer for knowledge and healing through the storms of your life. Give thanks and pray from the north.

Move to the center of your circle and face the lake. Place the blanket on the ground, raise your hands up high into the air, and pray. Pray from the center of your self.

Now sit in the center of your circle, facing the lake. Allow yourself to peer out at the water. Go inside and ask yourself, "What does this lake mean to me?" From within this self mask ask, "What does this beauty mean to me? What do my unspoken deaths and transitions in life mean to me now?"

Take time in the silence to meditate on the mirrorlike surface of the lake.

(Pause)

Now feel and trust yourself within your self mask. Listen a moment for any messages that come. Stand up, and allow yourself to begin to move freely on your blanket and around the circle. This is the dance of calling in your power animal. Say a prayer as you dance, and call up the image in your mind's eye of your power animal. Bring your power animal toward you in spirit and in reality. If you do not have a power animal, let one come to you now. Use your imagination and remember that what you imagine is real. Dance now, the dance that will help you call your power animal. Do not doubt what you see.

Take some time.

See your power animal with you in the circle. See your power animal dancing in its own way. See your power animal merging with you, your dances becoming one. In your own time, begin to slow your dance, and sit in your circle with your power animal. You feel strong within your self mask. You feel the healthy presence of your power animal. Take time now to be with your power animal and share the silence.

Now begin a dialogue with your power animal. Your power animal has come to bring you information, to bring you messages. Your power animal has come to meet you, as you wear your ancient self mask. What does your power animal have to say to you? What does your power animal give you? What do you give your power animal? Let there be a true healing talk between you. Use all your senses; intuit; commune with your power animal. Have this dialogue in the silence now.

When you have finished talking with your power animal, be silent once again. Then make a promise, a promise of action, to your power animal. There is something you are to do in order to own and bring into your waking life this self that you find within the self mask. So listen closely and hear your self tell your power animal what your promise of action will be. You will carry out this promise in your waking life. It may be very simple. You may be able to accomplish it in a day, in a moment. It may be something that you

do forever. It may be something that you must work on steadily for a time but that you will finish.

And now, giving thanks in your own way, embrace your power animal. Feel your self merging with your power animal as you embrace within the self mask, within your being. Have your power animal sit beside you. Know that the wise person within you is always nearby if you will only remember to draw on that strength.

Now you will begin to call people into your circle. First, bring the spirit of your mother into the circle. Give a prayer of thanks for however wonderful or difficult your relationship is or has been with your mother, and bring her spirit, her energy, her being into your circle. Your mother has a message for you as you wear your self mask. Come, have a dialogue with your mother. Allow her to join the circle. Allow more healing to take place between you and your mother. Take time in the silence, and listen to the message that your mother brings you, as you sit in your power circle.

What does your mother have to say about your mask? What is her teaching for you? What is her warning? What is her wisdom? Listen, hear, give thanks, trust.

Now embrace your mother. Let go of any difficulties you may have in doing this. Feel the healing. Sense the healing, and give thanks. If you have never known your mother or if you and she have become disconnected, reconnect with her now, in spirit, in energy, in love. And then let your mother leave the circle. As she does so, she moves sunwise around the lake until she is no longer with you, except in your heart.

Now say a prayer of thanks, and call into your circle your father. Feel your father; sense him. Trust that his most loving spirit, his most loving kindness and energy are available to you now. Bring your father in. Have a dialogue with him. Ask your father what he feels about you, what he feels about you from within your self mask. Listen to what he has to say. Take time in the silence now to be with your father, using all your senses to come closer, to break through any barriers you have had in the past. Take time in the silence now to talk with your father.

Take some time.

And now embrace your father. Hear him give thanks for you. You give thanks for him. Then thank your father, and see him leave the circle sunwise and move around the lake until he can no longer be seen, only felt in your heart and mind, spirit and soul.

Call in the energy now of your husband or wife, lover or best friend. Call this person in, and give thanks as you feel his or her spirit come into the circle. Take time in the silence to be with this person. This person, too, has a message for you. Ask this person questions. Have a dialogue. What does this person feel about you as you wear your ancient self mask? What has this person come to teach you? What sharing have you to do together? Take time in the silence to talk with your husband, wife, lover, or best friend. Listen, sense, feel, and hear, for there is a teaching that this person has come to give you. Hear and remember.

Take a moment.

And now embrace this person, merging with his or her energy, and allow this person to leave the circle sunwise and move around the lake.

Now I would like you to call in the spirit of a person who was once close to you but is no longer in your daily life. This may be a person who has died. This may be a person who has simply moved in a different direction and your lives no longer intersect. This is a person whom you have lost in one way or another. This is a person who was once dear, but something has changed. Call this person into your circle now. Trust whoever comes. Have a dialogue with this person. Feel his or her energy. Sense what this person has to tell you. What does he or she think and feel about you as you sit within the circle of your self mask? Trust that there is a message that this person has come to bring, and trust that he or she is a teacher for you, as are all the others who have come into this circle. Trust that this person can be brought back into your life as a teacher, just as you can reclaim parts of yourself as a teacher. Listen in the silence and talk with this lost person who is now found.

Take some time.

Now, embrace this person, feeling and sensing and trusting. Give thanks. Let the person leave the circle, moving sunwise around the lake, and know that this person will never disappear again, but will always be part of your inner world, your active world. Know that this person's energy, wisdom, love, and caring are real.

And now take time, as you sit in the circle with your power animal, just to be quiet. Think, reflect, be still. And now, as you sit with your power animal, embrace once more. Hear anything that you need to hear from your power animal. Ask any question. Listen. What message does your power animal have to tell you from within your self mask, for the wearing of this self mask, for the work to be done?

Take some time, in the silence, to do this.

Now give thanks and say good-bye to your power animal. Embrace, and see your power animal leave the circle sunwise and head out around the lake. Know that your power animal is never really separate from you, just as the energies of your mother and father, husband, wife, lover, and any of the lost ones are still with you inside.

But now you are alone in your circle within your ancient self mask. I would like you to stand up in your mind's eye and, moving to the center of the circle, take off your clothes and put them on the blanket. Then move out of the circle, sunwise, leaving by the east door, and move quickly to the lake, running, running, running quickly, and dive into the water. Feel your spirit energy soar. Feel your body come alive, as you cleanse yourself in the healing waters of the lake. It is cool but not too cool, and you swim and splash and dive deep. You realize that you still have your self mask on, and you are cleansed, and it is fine. Swim in the lake for a few moments. Float on your back. Dive deep into the water. Listen, and hear any messages that come as you cleanse yourself in the pure healing water of the lake.

Now come back on shore. Notice that your body grows warm as soon as you come out of the lake. The sun seems to dry it magically, quickly. Enter your circle from the east, and put your clothes back on. Stand in the center of your circle, and give thanks in silence. Give thanks for the teachings that you have learned, for the people who have come, for your power animal. Give thanks for yourself and your daily waking life.

And now from within your self mask, allow yourself, tell your-self, that you will learn whatever you need to learn, practice what-ever you need to practice, do whatever you need to do, in order to learn more and to fulfill your promise of action and to carry out any teachings you have learned from this meditation. Give thanks now, and take time in the silence to be within your circle.

Begin now to dismantle your circle so that you leave no trace in this wilderness place. Know that you can return to this lake at any time and that you can build a circle here at any time. Stone by stone you dismantle the circle, starting with the stones between the direc-tions, scattering them in the forest. And then you return the marker stones to the forest. The last thing you do is remove your self mask and wrap it in red natural material. Take it with you. Take time in the silence to do this now, moving mindfully and prayerfully.

(Pause)

When you have finished, allow the vision of this forest and lake to be clear in your mind's eye. Know that you can return here. Know that you will return here if and when it is necessary. Now turn from the lake in thanks, and begin walking back through the forest, conscious of each step, solid yet light, until soon you begin to place your consciousness back on your body and feel your feet on the ground. Feel your hands. Become aware of your breath, and notice how your breath rises and falls naturally, so that soon you are completely aware of your body, feeling grounded and solid within yourself. Whenever you are ready, in your own time, slowly begin to move your limbs, your neck, your hands, your legs and feet, becoming fully conscious of your body, and in your own time, open your eyes, and come back into the room.

WORKSHEET

Describe the lake and the place you chose for your ceremony. What do they mean to you?

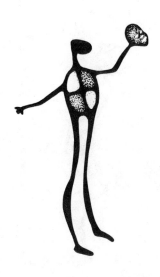

Describe the ancient mask you found. What about this mask represents your essence? How did you feel when you put it over your face?

Describe the dialogue and feelings you had when your power animal came to you. What promise of action did you make to your power animal?

What question did you have for your power animal? What was its message for you?

What message did your mother have for you? Your father?

What lessons did you learn from your husband or wife, lover or best friend?

What person who is no longer close to you did you call into your circle? What was his or her teaching?

What are the self wounds that you need to heal so that you may move farther down your path of heart?

PRAYER FOR THE FALSE FACE

I am a wise one.
I come from the faraway,
And I can lead you there.

I walk with the winds.
I am an important one.
I cling to the life of the spirit.

I am a false face healer.
I walk with the power of the sun
Around the mysteries of life.

I heal the mind and the heart.
I am an important one.
I am a being of sacred words.

I unravel the mysteries of your pain
So that you may find courage.
I heal the mind and the heart.

May you learn to follow the sacred ways.

I am of the light and the holy ones.
I walk in the land of spirit,
And I walk on the earth.

I honor all that is sacred.
Ho.

CHAPTER 3

HOW
TO MAKE
YOUR MASK

INTRODUCTION

As you make your shaman face of power, moving along your path of heart, there are several steps you must take. First, you must pray to the Great Spirit for guidance and understanding, and give thanks for your ability to learn. Second, you must identify the personas that have been a part of your life for so long, the personas that are most likely false faces that you have worn in society to protect yourself, to do what you think enhances your power but what really drains your power away. When you have identified those masks that no longer serve you, then you must move into the realm of the dream world or the subconscious through the process of visualization, and meet the dark side of yourself that you have so carefully hidden and avoided throughout your life. When you meet those aspects that are so often negative, you can find the source of their power, where they live in your body, and define what names they have in your life. You need to change those false faces, tearing them away from your original nature and, I hope, discarding them. This prepares you for your newly created "true face," a face that you can wear in your daily life and that will become a face of integrity for you. You will no longer need to hide behind various false personas. You will be able to begin living your medicine and living your truth in the world. Then and only then are you ready to discover your shaman face.

The shaman face is your face of power, the face of power that is used in ceremony when you are healing someone, when you are working with your altar (if you choose to do so), or when you are invoking the different energies of the universe in your own self-generated ceremonies that will bring power and magic and beauty into your life. Most of us are not Native American. We are not following a native tradition where very specific rituals are enacted. We are in a struggle to tear away the veils of ignorance that are destroying us and this great Mother Earth on which we live. We are searching for ways to empower ourselves in our daily lives. As I have learned from the Sisterhood of the Shields, discovering the shaman face of power that lives in the center of your altar is one very important way to empower yourself, for your altar is a microcosm of all the elements of strength and wisdom that you use in your waking life and in your sacred dream life.

Your shaman face of power enables you to create your own rainbow bridge between your everyday life in society and the spirit world, the world of power that lives all around you within the mystery. The shaman face will help you to access what is real but what you cannot see and what cannot be explained with the rational mind. The power of light can only be lived with an open heart and the truth of your being.

So, as you begin to build your mask, you will build first an exact replica of your own face; then you will take this replica and perform a ceremony in the wilderness, planting your face into the earth from whence it came, leaving it there overnight to be empowered by Mother Earth, the stars, and the universe. Then your face, in essence, will be reborn from the earth, given to you by the power of Mother Earth into your hands, to be empowered with your own unique symbols and colors and imbued with your dance of power so that you make the energy of this mask stand up and live and become a part of your sacred world.

I honor your commitment to this journey, and I send you down your path with love and with spirit.

Upon completion of the two-day "Face of the Earth" ceremony, described in the next chapter, you will return to decorate your mask. As you do so, remember that you have both an inner and an outer face. Remember the four directions of your mask, and handle your mask with respect. Know that this process is like peeling away the layers of an onion—you may feel open and exposed. This feeling is part of the process.

When decorating, use materials that symbolize what you saw in your meditations and the emotions you experienced. Be sure to represent your power animal on your mask. Acrylic paints work wonderfully. Colored pencils and crayons can also be used. Feathers, beads, small pouches of herbs or tobacco, and other objects can be attached to the mask. For best results, anything heavier than a feather should be affixed with a glue gun.

Your mask is your sacred shaman face. Honor and respect it. Make an offering to Mother Earth, giving thanks for her wisdom and guidance and for the materials that you have used in this process of mask making.

DIRECTIONS FOR MAKING YOUR MASK

What you will need to make your mask:

1. Plaster-impregnated gauze
2. A pair of scissors
3. A bowl filled with warm water
4. Petroleum jelly
5. An old towel and headband or scarf (to hold hair back)
6. A smudge stick and matches
7. A mirror (if you are making your own mask)
8. Acrylic gesso and paintbrushes
9. Feathers, beads, small mirrors, paints (or anything else to use as decoration)

The plaster-impregnated gauze, called "Rigid Wrap," can be purchased at crafts stores for about $3 per roll. You can also find the gauze at hospital supply outlets, under the name "Johnson & Johnson Specialist Plaster Bandages"; in these stores, it sells for about $30 for twelve rolls. One roll will be enough to make one mask.

You can make masks by yourself, using a mirror, or with a partner. The process of mask making is a meditation. Consider smudging yourself, your partner, the materials to be used, and the area in which you will be working with burning sage before you begin the process. Play soothing, meditative music in the background. You may want to surround the area with white light or work inside a protective circle of tobacco. Trust yourself and do what feels right. Work in silence, and respect the process you have begun.

Before applying the gauze, decide whether you want your eyes and mouth open or closed. Close your eyes. Open your eyes. Which feels more expressive to you at the moment? Close your mouth. Open your mouth. Which speaks more loudly? Listen to your thoughts and emotions during this part of the process. Are you afraid of covering your eyes or of opening your mouth? What does this say about you? Everything that happens in this process is meant to be. When you allow yourself, you will understand the deeper meaning.

Follow the step-by-step directions on pages 68 to 71 for making the mask. When you have completed them, let the mask dry. You may want to place the mask in the sun or near a source of heat. When the mask is completely dry, paint the front and back with white acrylic gesso. Gesso may be found at any arts and crafts supply store. The gesso makes your mask more durable and can repair structural damage or weaknesses in the mask. Hold your mask up to the light to see where you may need to apply more gesso. Let your mask dry thoroughly and completely.

MASK-MAKING INSTRUCTIONS

Cut gauze into 24 ¾″ by 5″ strips. You may need to trim some of the strips into smaller pieces as you go along.

Wrap an old towel around your shoulders to protect your clothing, and tie back your hair. Liberally apply petroleum jelly (Vaseline, for example) to your entire face. Be certain to cover completely your eyebrows, eyelashes, and hairline.

Thoroughly immerse the strips of gauze in a bowl of warm water. Be sure that they are wet before applying them to your face.

Begin to apply gauze strips around the outside of your face (in a ring), allowing the strips to overlap by about ½".

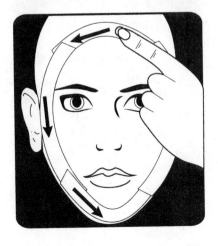

Using wet fingertips, smooth out the strips and mold them to your face. Remember to dip fingers in warm water periodically to keep them wet.

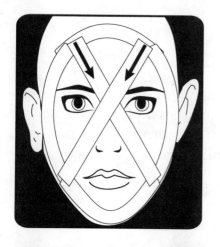

Cross two strips over the bridge of your nose, allowing X to overlap with outer strips by ½″ at hairline and jawline. Remember to smooth out the strips with wet fingertips.

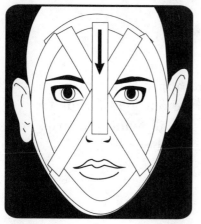

Lay one gauze strip straight down the center of your forehead to the tip of your nose, again overlapping with outer strips by ½″ at hairline.

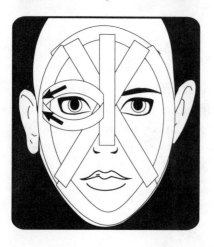

Frame eyes with smaller strips, allowing the gauze to follow the natural arch of the eye and again overlapping the strips.

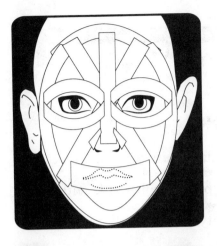

Place small strip over mouth and around nostrils. *Be sure to leave nostrils open.* (If you want an open-mouth mask, apply small strips around mouth as you did around eyes.)

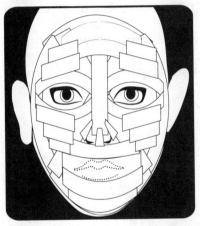

Now fill in the mask. Working symmetrically from outside of face inward, apply a second layer to all but the nose and mouth.

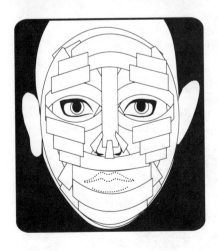

Allow mask to dry. Lift mask off face by scrunching face to loosen the edges. Hold the mask to the light to look for any air holes. Patch holes with short strips of gauze.

Note: When you clean up, be sure not to put used plaster water down the drain.

POWER SONG

Create a power song to call your tutelary spirits, your ancestors, your power animal, or any of the other beings you work with in the Dreamtime. Your power song can simply be several lines of "I Am, I Am, I Am." Or it can be a short poem in song form. It can be written in any way that is meaningful and powerful for you. It must be expressive of the essence, soul, and power of your being and must be easy to remember.

CHAPTER 4

THE
FACE OF
THE EARTH

FIRST DAY

INTRODUCTION

This is a two-day ceremony. On the first day you will take your mask of your own face to a wilderness area where you will place your "face," or mask, into the earth. Through this ceremony with Mother Earth, you will give away pain, addictions, and whatever else you are finished with in your life. You will write and sing your power song for your mask.

With your mask placed in the earth, you will see that you are actually the "face of the earth." Then, when you build your altar, you will be able to build it as though it were your face looking up out of Mother Earth with the full essence of your being.

This ceremony is to be performed toward sunset—the time when the face of the earth changes. You should bring these items:

Your undecorated mask
Sacred things important to you
Tobacco
A small, scarf-sized cloth of red, made of natural fibers
Sage and matches
A small blanket or cloth to sit on
Your power song
Your personal pipe (optional)

CEREMONY/MEDITATION

Close your eyes and move into your shaman center. Follow your breath for a moment.

Mother Earth talks to us of the truth of our being. She always gives us a face that is true. She creates a reflection in the trees, in the lakes and the rivers, in the oceans, in the mountains, and in the meadows. She creates a reflection of perfection and beauty that cannot be denied. If we are sensitive, it is hard sometimes to look into the mirrors that Mother Earth provides, because they make us aware of our own imperfection. But the beauty of the earth is also an everlasting inspiration.

The nineties are a decade for healing Mother Earth. To heal her, we must first heal ourselves. So much of what we have been going through in the last few years has to do with an internal death, transformation, and rebirth. We are changing at such an extraordinarily rapid pace that it is hard to keep up. These changes are truly a shock to our system. We are shedding the old—the old persona, the old faces that we have been wearing—but to manifest our true destiny in life, we have to choose our new face with great care. We must make

ourselves emotionally ready to wear that new persona. This ceremony is about coming into relationship with our true persona.

As our guide, Mother Earth presents us with her beautiful and
magnificent face, ever-changing but always real and true, a manifestation of the very essence of the mystery of life. Mother Earth in all
her beauty is the true expression of the face of the Goddess Mother.
Thus, when we call our altar the "face of the earth," we are actually
honoring the firstness of woman.

In keeping with this concept of the "face of the earth," we are
going to perform a ceremony with Mother Earth in which we take
the masks we have made of our own beautiful faces and place them
into the earth, giving our faces to the heart of the Great Mother,
seeing then that we actually are the face of the earth. For when you
build your altar, you build it as if it was actually your face, looking
up out of Mother Earth and expressing the full essence of your being.

The concept of "mask" is an ancient one, and it has to do with
drama, drama on every level of existence—from the tragicomic
drama of everyday life to the tragic and joyous comedy of shaman
endeavor, which has to do with life and death, rebirth and transformation, and the sacred dream. In making, decorating, and empow-

ering your mask, you must first know intimately the different aspects of yourself. You must know who you are, where your weaknesses are, and where your power lives. It is important to be intimately acquainted with the four directions. Keep in mind your personal symbols. Symbols are extraordinarily important and powerful in and of themselves. A symbol not only has its own power but it also represents other powers that are beyond words. As above, so below. When you have matter, you also have spirit. When you have spirit, you also have matter. One cannot exist without the other. A symbol is the physical counterpart, or explanation, for something that is more than words can describe. If you use the sun as a symbol, it represents the life giver. Without the sun, life could not exist. It represents the rise and fall of our emotions and of our destiny. The sun represents power. The sun often represents male energy. It represents the cycles of life and so much more. To each person the sun means something a little bit different. That is why symbols are so important. Each symbol represents something that is essential to your makeup as a human being.

In this process of healing the body of Mother Earth, we must search deep in our souls in the next few years to understand what

Mother Earth symbolizes to us. How does she affect you? How do you affect her? What is the relationship of your own integrity as a person to the integrity of Mother Earth? When you plant your mask into Mother Earth and make your first real face of the earth altar, you need to remember that this is not a ritual. The ceremony of the face of the earth is just that—it is a ceremony. A ceremony is different from a ritual. It can be different every time you do it, because there is a piece of you in this ceremony that is self-generated, that makes this ceremony different from each and every other one that is being created. A ritual never changes. It is performed by rote.

However, it is still important, even in this ceremony, to do a few specific things. The first thing is to make your mask, leaving it open and with no decoration. Then take it out into a wilderness area and find a place of power for you—a place where you feel strong, at ease, and warm. Once you have found this place, look around you with your truest vision. Be aware of the directions around you; be aware of the wind, of whatever birds fly over, and of any animals that you see. Then, moving clockwise, make a sacred circle with tobacco, a circle that is large enough for you to sit in. You have brought whatever sacred things are important to you, as well as your mask and some sage. You have brought a piece of natural-fiber red material with you. Now gather your marker stones for the four directions.

After placing these stones for the south, west, north, and east, say a prayer for protection, and enter the circle by the east door. Sit within your circle, facing west. Sit on a blanket of any kind, a very small one, or a little piece of cloth, something that sets you apart and makes the center of the circle sacred and special. Then dig a small indentation in the earth, just large enough to hold your mask. When you have dug the hole, clear it out carefully, and place your red material in the bottom of the hole. Then place sage over that, and place your mask face down, facing the heart of Mother Earth. Be sure that your mask is comfortable, facing down into the earth.

Now it is time to gather the stones that represent what you want to give away, what you are truly done with in life—pains, addictions, worries, problems. Take time as you gather them and contemplate carefully what you are giving away. When you have chosen these stones, reenter your sacred circle from the east and sit down in the center. Hold the stones up to the Great Spirit, and say something like this:

Great Spirit, Mother Earth, powers of the four directions, my medicine, my allies, my ancestors, and all those who love me, hear me now. This is a ceremony for my false face, so that I may build my shaman power mask for all time.

It is now that you sing your power song. When you have sung your power song, take your stones and place them, beginning in the south, around the perimeter of your mask. Take a lot of time with this. Think deeply about the things that you want to give away—things that you are through with, things that have been a block to your sacred life and to the manifestation of your true destiny. Contemplate each stone as you place it near your mask until you have completed the circle.

When you have finished, say a prayer to the Great Spirit, to Mother Earth, to your guardians, and to your allies. Always speak to the Great Spirit first. Talk about the power that you want to bring to this mask, your new persona, your shaman face. You must pray, and pray well.

I will give you an idea of the sort of prayer that I used when I woke up my mask. Although this is not a ceremony to awaken your mask, it represents the beginning of that journey.

I am a shaman woman.
I am a false face magician.
I come from the faraway.
I am a woman of words.

With this face I will heal.
With this new face,
I will bring joy into the world.

I am a woman of words.
I am a shaman woman.
I am spirit woman.
I come from the faraway.

I bring waves to the water
And wind to the trees.
I heal the mind and the heart.

With this face,
I see you.

With these new eyes,
I see you.

I am four eyes now,
For I have my new shaman face.
Ho!

As you say this invocation of power, draw a crescent moon in the sand or dirt to the left of your mask, and on the right, draw the sun. Above your mask, draw a six-pointed star. And at the bottom, below your mask, draw a pyramid. Then with all the emotion that you can muster from your heart, from your life, from that part of you that wants so desperately to find truth and what is real and that part of you that understands the sacredness of Mother Earth, the sacredness of the powers that be, turn your mask over, placing one hand on the left and one on the right and then simply pulling the left side up and over so that now your face is looking out of Mother Earth and up to Father Sky. Fill in the sand or dirt around the face so that it is as if it were a stone, sitting on the floor of the desert that has always been there. Now take sage, cedar, or sweetgrass and bless your mask; smudge your mask and yourself. And pray. Pray in your own way.

As you perform this ceremony, know that this is the beginning of your new persona in the world. Do what is needed to bring power into your circle. For example, this is a beautiful time to smoke your pipe, if you have one.

Now leave your circle by the east door, this time closing it behind you with tobacco to protect your mask and saying a prayer of protection. I say something like this, "I place an aura of divine love around this circle so that it is protected from all harm. Ho."

Then walk in silence and beauty, as quietly as you know how, carefully placing each footstep onto the ground so that you disturb the earth very little.

Pray with your pipe, sing, drum, or do whatever is sacred and appropriate for you. If you are performing this ceremony at home or in your backyard, observe the night in a sacred way. It would be appropriate to fast or to eat only lightly.

SECOND DAY

INTRODUCTION

You will perform this part of the ceremony on the second day near dawn. You will return to find your face, or mask, in the earth. You will gather it up and return to the place where your mask decorating will begin.

CEREMONY/MEDITATION

When you return to the sacred place you chose the day before, kneel before your circle, before your face looking up from the earth. Make offerings of tobacco or herbs. Let the Great Spirit hear your voice to see if it is true.

Sing your power song now, and invoke the powers of the four directions. Then enter your circle by the east door, and sit before your placid face. In your open face see the manifestation of all possibilities. Meditate with your self about your acts of power. Meditate on what you are and who you will become. You are of Mother Earth, and to the earth you will one day return.

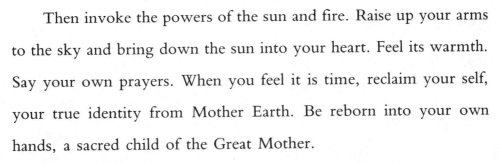

Then invoke the powers of the sun and fire. Raise up your arms to the sky and bring down the sun into your heart. Feel its warmth. Say your own prayers. When you feel it is time, reclaim your self, your true identity from Mother Earth. Be reborn into your own hands, a sacred child of the Great Mother.

Place your mask on your lap, fold the sage inside the red cloth, and carry this bundle inside your mask. Smooth the ground with your hands, and leave your circle by the east door.

Walk now with your gait of power back to the place where the mask decorating will begin.

WORKSHEET

Write down your power song.

Describe your emotions as you perform this ceremony.

What do the stones represent for you in this ceremony?

What did you give away that may have been a block to your sacred life? What pain, problems, addictions? Describe your feelings as you gave each away.

Where does the female place of power live in your body? What does it feel like?

Where does the male place of power live in your body? What does it feel like?

What was your wilderness place like? What kinds of birds flew over? From what direction? What animals did you see? From which direction did the wind blow?

CHAPTER 5

MASKS
AND
PERSONAS

INTRODUCTION

To discover your true face of power, you must first go through a rigorous and tireless process of letting go of old habits, addictions, and negativity. Each of us has some form of addiction that we must deal with. This meditation leads you to the source of your powerlessness and addictive behavior.

EXERCISE/MEDITATION

Let yourself relax by beginning to focus on your breath. Your mind rests when breath is your focus. Remember always that breath is the guide to inner peace. Breathe slowly and naturally. Let your breath drop down into your belly, into the center of your being. Here you can begin to still the confusions, worries, or problems of your daily life, and you can begin to realize that most solutions to outer problems come through inner work.

As you allow your breath to be your focus, gradually become aware of your body. Feel your body. Let your body be full of light, for breath is light; it is the pathway to healing.

In our life we wear many masks, many faces each day. Today, before you begin your journey, let these masks drop. Let yourself be

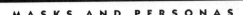
still in the silence as you begin to become more and more deeply relaxed. Now, place your consciousness on your body. Become aware of your feet. Visualize your feet touching the ground firmly yet gently. Allow yourself to feel the bottoms of your feet, and imagine that they are roots that go down deep into the earth, grounding you there. Relax your feet. Relax your ankles, too. Feel free at any time to move in the direction of greater comfort and joy. If you feel tension or pain, let yourself relax with that. Let any sounds you hear become part of your relaxation. In our world we move so far away from relaxation that it is difficult to get our bearings. Allow your calves and your lower legs to relax. Relax your knees and the backs of your knees. Breathe down through your body; allow your breath to move down through your body to your feet. Relax your thighs. Relax your sexual center. Relax your buttocks and your hips. Do not let yourself stray from relaxation. Trust your body as we begin to go inside. Now relax your midsection, your belly. Imagine that the muscles, the organs, of your midsection are all relaxing, just lightening up a little, doing their work a little better, a little more easily. And now, as you continue breathing slowly and naturally, relax your lungs, relax your chest, and imagine even your heart

relaxing. Take a moment now to give thanks as you are relaxing. Give thanks in the silence.

Now, breathing slowly, relax your neck and throat, allowing your throat to feel open—the pathway to expression being cleared. Relax your shoulders. So many of us carry the weight of the world on our shoulders. Let this weight drop now. Allow your breath to help you relax your arms and hands, your fingers, and your facial muscles. Let the back of your neck feel free. Let the muscles behind your eyes gently relax, and the top of your scalp also, so that soon your whole body is deeply and gently quiet. You feel very calm and gentle. You feel at home in your body. Each breath is like a wave of kindness that calms you and radiates out from your body.

And now that you are quiet, fully alert yet deeply relaxed, we are going to take a journey. I said that there are many masks that we wear every day. On our journey, we are going to work with these masks. Focus once again on your breathing, letting your breath drop down, deep into the center of your being. And in your mind's eye, in your imagination, in your own way, I would like you to imagine a wilderness place. This place may be a desert, a forest, the ocean

shore, or the chaparral. Allow yourself to see, to feel, to sense in your own way a wilderness place. In your imagination, bring this place to you. Bring yourself to this place, for this is a place of inner peace and inner strength and power.

(Pause a moment.)

See or feel or sense yourself walking in this wilderness place. There is no one else here, yet you do not feel afraid or lonely. You feel strength in the quiet solitude of the wilderness. Your body is charged with relaxation and calm, with a sense of purpose and a power that is your own. As you walk in this wilderness place, begin to notice the colors, any flowers that you might see, trees or bushes. Notice sounds, the way the wind feels, the sound of birds flying. Let yourself walk until you come to a place that feels just right. It is here that you find your cave. It is hidden among the rocks and behind the trees. This place feels like home to you. In your imagination, take a moment to find stones around this cave that speak to you, that are magically nearby, to build a sacred circle just inside the cave. Place one stone at the east, one at the south, one at the west, and one at the north.

Take a moment.

And now that you have built your circle, stand at the south stone, and take a moment in silence to say a prayer, a prayer of thanks for all the gifts you have received in your life. Then walk around the outside of the circle, and entering from the south, walk around it from the south to the west to the north to the east.

It is difficult to see in the shadowed darkness of the cave. You find a torch wedged into the wall, and you light it with a match. With a flash of brilliant yellow flame, the entire interior of the cave comes alive. Magnificent masks of every description hang on the cave walls, from the floor to the rocky ceiling. Red, yellow, blue, white designs and symbols are painted on grotesque and beautiful faces. Snarling, meek, and ferocious animal faces, the personas of human magic, lend their power and personality to your sacred cave. You look carefully at each one, marveling at the intricacy of their design. You begin to realize that these masks are representative of your many lives and emotions.

You then sit in the center facing south in your sacred circle. The south is the place of trust and innocence, and here in this cave of masks, you will meet the faces of your child within. Spread a blanket out before you in the south. On this blanket will soon appear masks for the different faces of the child within you, the different energies, the different qualities, for really there are many children within you—remnants of the child you were and energies of the child you still are.

Now see before you a mask of the playful child within you, and feel joy inside you. Notice the smile come to your face as you see this mask appear. Look at the mask, and see the joy in the mask, and feel the joy inside you begin to grow as you pick up the mask of the playful child. Place this mask over your face, and be silent. Notice now how this mask feels. Do you want to dance, run, play ball, laugh? Trust that images of this playful child may appear in your mind's eye as you wear the mask; allow all of these images to arise. Go deeply inside yourself, your playful child self.

Now listen quietly, listen in the silence of this wilderness cave, in the silence of your heart and mind and body, and get a message from your playful child within, a message, a sign, a statement that gives you help, that allows you to bring this child forth more and more in your life in appropriate ways. Allow yourself to breathe deeply with this mask, with this power of play. Listen now in the silence for the message, and remember. Remember, for each of us has lost much of our playfulness, much of our joy, much of our spontaneity, our deep, deep pleasure and laughter. So listen and re-member, and when you are done, take the thumb and forefinger of your right hand and touch them together, locking in the energy, the playfulness, the memory, so that in the future you may bring back this message and honor your playful child within in your daily life.

(Pause)

Now replace the mask on the blanket, and find there in front of you another mask, a different mask, one that we need to be more conscious of. This is the mask of your abandoned child within. Pick up this mask, and place it on your face, noticing what it looks like,

the possible fear or pain or sadness in the mask. Become conscious that you live out this abandoned child in many ways, and by knowing its qualities, its message, its energy, you can free yourself from the feelings of abandonment and begin to take care of this pain yourself. You can mother yourself. So, placing the mask over your face, feel the energy, feel the sadness and pain of your abandonment early in life, for all of us have been abandoned in many ways. We have been let down. We did not receive what we needed from our parents because they did not have everything that we needed. Allow yourself to feel your abandoned child within, and let yourself know that by being aware of it and feeling your emotions from this place, you can begin to let them go or to honor them when they come up, to give this child time to heal. So now, in the silence within the mask of your abandoned child, listen, and receive a message. Pay attention to any images that might come while you are wearing this mask. Trust that they are signs and teachers for you, and listen for a message from your abandoned child, and remember. How does this abandoned child control your life? How does this child restrict you?

(Pause)

Now place the thumb and forefinger of your right hand together so that you will remember and honor the message of abandonment, because when we honor this energy in our daily lives, we give ourselves a chance to heal through greater awareness.

Now replace that mask on the altar, and pick up the mask you see before you of the creative child within you. Feel the power in this child. It is different from the power of the playful child. There is a deepness, a strength that emanates from this child. Pick up this mask and place it over your face. Feel the energy that surges through you. Let any images come from your childhood. Honor them by giving thanks.

How does this mask feel? Pay attention to your feelings. Trust whatever you are feeling. Go deep inside the spirit of your creative child so that you will know and receive a message, and you will remember this message. Take time in the silence to become one with the creative child. Has this creative child been expressed in your life? There may be something this child wants you to do. What is it? Trust that it is good and that whatever message comes is a healing one.

(Pause)

When you have received your message, place the thumb and forefinger of your right hand together, anchoring in that memory, anchoring in that knowledge, anchoring in that healing.

Now take the mask off and replace it on the altar, and pick up one more mask. This is the mask of the vulnerable child. Many of us wear this mask often in our daily lives as adults. Feel the fear in this mask as you pick it up—yet there may also be kindness, an ability to care, and an openness. Vulnerability is often a power in its own right. It can teach us wisdom; it can teach us to be whole and open.

So place this mask over your face, and feel your vulnerability. Feel your vulnerable child, and go inside the silence. Go inside and become this vulnerable child. Let any feelings or images appear. Trust them. Is there anything you are supposed to do? Is there anything your vulnerable child is supposed to do? How does the vulnerable child feel about your power? Listen and remember. Take time in the silence to get a message from your vulnerable child. We bring this child up to consciousness so that we can live our lives with meaning and awareness of the many selves that we are.

(Pause)

After you have received your message, anchor it in by touching your thumb and forefinger of your right hand together firmly and gently. Know that you will remember what you need to remember in order to bring your vulnerable child up into awareness, so that you do not live your life unconsciously.

Now take the mask off and replace it on the altar of your blanket. Say a prayer in silence, and give thanks for the trust and innocence of the south, of your child within, to your many children within. Give thanks and pray that you may take care of yourself, that you may love yourself enough to trust and honor your inner wisdom, your inner child, your inner children.

Take a moment.

Now move to the west stone, the place of dreams, the place of introspection, the place of the darkness inside each of us, the place of the woman inside each of us, the place of looking within, the place of going away and being still and quiet. Turn to the west and say a prayer. Let yourself pray for guidance, and give thanks as you turn around the sacred wheel that you are becoming more and more aware of the depths of yourself, of the multiplicity of selves that reside in each of us.

Facing west, place a blanket inside the circle, a blanket that will be your west altar. Here you will put on the masks of your adolescent self.

See on the blanket the mask of fear. Notice how this mask looks to you. Is it contorted, shy, withdrawn, pulling away? Take this mask in your hands, and place it on your face. When you have the mask on, feel the depth of your fear. Feel the depth of your adolescent fear, your fear as a young person. If you can know your own fear, fear can be a teacher for you. The poet James Wright said, "Fear is what quickens me." So feel and sense your fear, and let any images come to you as you live within the mask of fear.

Now get an image and a message. Find a message that will come to you from your mask of fear, a message that will be a teaching, a gift, so that fear does not run your life but acts only as a teacher to help you. Name your fear. Is it a fear of death, fear of success, fear of loneliness? Take time in the silence to get a message from within this mask of fear, from within your body as it lives within this mask.

Take some time.

When you have gotten the message, take the thumb and fore-finger of your right hand and place them together, anchoring in this message so that you will remember what you need to remember from within this mask of fear.

Now remove the mask of fear, and place it back on the altar. Pick up another mask you find there—the mask of anger, the anger of not knowing, the anger of limitations, the anger of frustrations, the anger of early loss. Place this mask on your face, noticing as you do what this mask looks like—the rigidity, perhaps, or the strength, the sense of being out of control. Notice whatever is in this mask of anger, and after you have the mask placed on your face, feel, sense, be this adolescent anger that still resides within you. Pay attention to any images that may come. Pay attention, and listen for a message, a teaching from this mask of anger, so that we may become more conscious of our anger, the residual anger from our adolescence that lives in us now. And as we become more conscious of this aspect of our many selves, we will no longer allow ourselves to be run by anger unconsciously.

Listen now in the silence for a message from anger in the west of your adolescence. What was your greatest source of anger in adolescence? Trust the message that comes. Remember the message that comes.

Take some time.

Place your thumb and forefinger together, anchoring in the message so that, once again, you will remember what you need to remember, and you will receive this gift from anger in the west, a gift that you may use in your daily life.

Now take off the mask of anger, and place it back on the altar of the west. Take a new mask. This mask is the mask of your hidden self, the part that was locked away in adolescence, the part of you that is unknown even to yourself. As you pick up the mask, notice how it looks. It will probably look very different for each of you, for what is hidden inside each of us is ours alone, and as we become more in touch with what is hidden, we take ourselves out of the darkness and move into the light. Take this mask of the hidden self, and place it over your face, allowing yourself to feel and sense and be aware of any images that may come, that may be living inside this mask of the hidden self. Trust the unknown, and again, listen in the silence for a message that comes to you from the place of the hidden self. What is the self that is struggling to be born?

Take time.

After you have received this message, place your thumb and forefinger together, anchoring in the message, knowing that you will remember and be able to return to and learn more from any of these masks and any of these places around the sacred wheel.

Now replace the mask of the hidden self on the altar, and pick up a new mask. Pick up the mask of the rebel, and feel the fire in this mask; feel the pain in this mask—the mask of the outsider, the mask of the one who resists and struggles, the mask of one who is not at home in his or her environment. Notice the mask as you hold it in your hands, and then place the mask of the rebel over your face. Take

time in the silence to feel this mask, to feel its power, to feel its weakness, to feel yourself powerful and weak at the same time. Sense and feel and trust from within this mask that there is a teaching here, and take time in the silence, once again, to receive a message from this mask of the rebel.

Take some time.

When you have received your message, place your thumb and forefinger together, and anchor in this message, this truth, this wisdom, this intuition that is coming to you through the mask of the rebel.

Next, see one more mask on the altar of the west, on the altar of the adolescent self within. This is a mask of love, a mask of young love, a mask of pure love. Notice the beauty of this mask as you hold it in your hands. Notice its calmness; notice any fear that may be there. Sense and feel and allow any images to come as you place this mask over your face, breathing within the mask of love. Take time in the silence as you feel yourself and sense and wait for images or call images to you of times when you felt love. How different is it for you to receive love rather than give it? Take time in the silence to hear a message that will come to you through the mask of love.

Take some time.

Now take your thumb and forefinger of your right hand and place them together, anchoring in this knowledge, this message, this teaching, from within the mask of love.

Replace the mask of love on the altar, and see all the masks sitting before you. Now from the west, from the place of intuition, of going within, from the place of dreams, the place of adolescence, say a prayer of thanks for the teachings that you have received. And say a prayer of thanks for the struggles and the joys that you have experienced in your adolescence in this life. Ask that your adolescence continue to be a teacher, a conscious teacher, as you allow it in its various guises of rebel, of love, of the hidden self, of anger, and of fear. So take time now in the silence to say a prayer of thanks.

Now move to face the north stone. Place a blanket in front of you as an altar to the spirit of the north. The north is the place of

wisdom, the place of work and of giving away your knowledge. The north is the place from which storms come and the place where we learn from our relationships and our difficulties. The north is the place also of the adult, and here you will put on the masks of your adult self, masks that you wear interchangeably every day, either consciously or unconsciously. Before we begin with the north and the adult masks, say a prayer of thanks for the teachings that you have had in your life, for the wisdom that you have shared with others, for the insights that are yet to come, and for the difficulties that you have had to endure.

Give thanks for what you have learned through these difficulties.

Now see before you, on the altar of the north, a mask that is the worker mask. Pick it up, look at it, see the tension in the face of the mask. See the joy; see the travail; see the deep lines of energy, symbolizing how much energy must be used in the name of work, in the face of work. Place the north mask, the worker mask, on your face, and allow any images to come of how it feels to be living inside this worker mask. Take time in the silence to become one with your worker self. There is a message that this mask can bring to you, perhaps a message about how to get more joy out of work, perhaps about how to reduce tension. It could be any message. How do you feel about your work? Is your work your act of power in this life? Trust that a message will come and that there will be a teaching for you in this mask, as you bring this worker self more and more to consciousness. So listen now in the silence for a message. Feel and sense a message coming.

(Pause)

When you have received your message, place your thumb and forefinger together, anchoring in this message, trusting that there is insight here. Sit a while in the silence with this insight, with this message, knowing and asking that more will be revealed to you as time goes on and as you choose to work and become one with this worker mask.

Now replace the worker mask on the altar of the north, and find there another mask. This is the mask of the lover. Pick it up. Sense, feel, think, and know what this mask means to you. Place the mask on your face, allowing any images to come, feeling the beauty, the sadness, the joy, the pain, all that is involved in being a lover. Trust that there is more work to do to become an even greater lover—a lover of your self, a lover of others, a lover able to be intimate, a lover of earth, a lover of all living things. Go into the silence from this place of the lover, from within this lover mask, and listen now for a message in the silence.

Take your time. Trust.

And now hear the message and put the thumb and forefinger of your right hand together, anchoring it in, knowing that more can be revealed later, telling yourself that you will remember, that you will learn, and you will grow. Use all your senses.

Replace the mask, taking it off your face and placing it back on the altar, giving thanks once again. Find before you another mask of your adult self. This mask is the mask of the critic. Pick up your critic mask. See it; feel it; sense it. Place the critic mask over your face. Notice whatever feelings you have, whatever tension, whatever strength. Allow yourself to feel, to sense, to go deeply inside the critic self. Let yourself be the critic. Many of us spend so much time living within our own critic. By becoming more conscious of our inner critic, we can learn to be aware of its strengths and its weaknesses, of its damage to us and its help to us.

Now, as you go inside as the critic, let yourself dream. Let yourself be aware of any images that come, any feelings. How does the critic feel about your actions in life? As you go inside, get a message, a statement, some information that the critic will give you to help you on your path of wholeness. How does the critic control your life? Does the critic approve of your vulnerable child?

Take a few minutes in silence to receive your message.

Now tell yourself that you will retain your message, that you will remember what you need to remember. Give thanks, as you take off your critic mask and replace it on the altar of the north.

See one more mask on the altar of the north. This is the mask of the unexpressed self. Notice its beauty. Notice any confusion. Notice the shy, withdrawn quality of this mask. Pick up this mask and place it over your face. Feel deeply the unused power, the quietness. There is a real strength that this mask holds. As you place this mask on your face, become one with it. Listen with your whole being to what your unexpressed self is trying to tell you. Take time in the silence to get a message, to receive, so that you may bring your unexpressed self into expression. What is it that you need to do? What is it that you are not accomplishing? Where do you need to spend more energy, time, love, joy? Take time in the silence to receive a message from your unexpressed self. Why have you not heard from her or him before?

(Pause)

Now allow yourself to give thanks, as you replace the mask of your unexpressed self back on the altar of the north. Give thanks to the shields of your adult self—the worker, the lover, the critic, and the unexpressed self. Let them go.

Turn now, and sit facing the east. The east is the place of illumination, the place of true creativity, the place of the trickster or heyoka. The east is the place of the sunrise, of new birth, new joy, new change and challenge. See before you a blanket that is an altar of the east, and pick up the mask that you see before you of the old wise one. This mask represents the grandfather or grandmother self. Take this mask and notice the power that resides in it. See the ancient beauty shining through the mask. Take this mask and place it over your face. Go deeply inside yourself. Listen for a message of wisdom from the old wise one. How does the old wise one feel about your act of power, about the way you are manifesting your dream in this life?

(Pause)

Now tell yourself that you will remember the message. Learn from it. As you place the mask back onto the altar, give thanks.

Now pick up the mask of the fool, the trickster. See the humor that is so necessary for our lives. Place the mask over your face. Burst forth from the mask. Go inside. Feel the wisdom in this mask. How does the trickster feel about your life up until now? Sense, feel, trust yourself as the fool. Sense, feel, and listen for a message.

Take a few minutes now in silence to do this.

Now remember what you need to remember. Become one with the fool so that the fool can come up in all its positive aspects, giving you humor and spontaneity, breaking up the dry conversations of life, giving you new insight, peace, and pleasure, causing joyous chaos. Now replace the fool mask on the altar and give thanks.

See one more mask on the altar of the east. This is the mask of fulfillment. Pick this one up and look at it carefully. As you place it over your face, understand that this mask may be one that you know little about. Sense, feel, touch, allow any images to come. Go deeply inside the mask of fulfillment, and feel yourself within this place. Feel grounded and solid. Feel strong and balanced. Feel contentment. Go inside and receive a message from within the mask of fulfillment, a message about your totality and your life. Then, remembering your message, replace the mask on the altar of the east, and give thanks.

(Pause)

Turn now and stand in the center of your circle. In the center is the Self. We move in all directions, but always at our center is our Self. We have many aspects of our being, but always in the center is our core, our Self, our sacred witness. Out of all the masks that you have put on, I would like you now to pick one to represent your Self. This may be the mask that is calling you most strongly. This may be the mask that you feel most at home with. This may be the mask that you will take the next few months to work with most directly. Out of all the masks that you have put on, pick one to represent your Self. Take a few moments in silence to think and sense and feel before you choose your mask.

(Pause)

Now that you have chosen your mask, place it over your face. Sit quietly in the center of your sacred circle. Say a prayer for your Self from within this mask. Say a prayer that you may become more knowledgeable from within this mask, from within this persona. Let the knowledge and the power and the wisdom to be learned from within this mask come directly into the center of your Self and merge. Go into your center now, and have a dialogue; listen for a message from this mask, from your Self within this mask. As you go inside, realize that you will work with this mask more strongly now

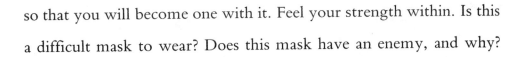

so that you will become one with it. Feel your strength within. Is this a difficult mask to wear? Does this mask have an enemy, and why?

Take time.

Remembering the message from this mask, take the mask off, and place it before you. Sitting in the center of your circle, take a few moments in silence to be, to focus on your body, to let any words of prayer well up from within you.

Breathe from your belly. Know that you have traveled a great distance on this journey and that there is much more ground to cover. But now is a good time to stop and relax in this wilderness cave and give thanks. And as you give thanks, let your sacred circle fade. Let the masks disappear. They are part of your Self, and you will remember them, and you will remember the messages so that you will work with these masks again. These masks will become part of your conscious mind, not just your unconscious, so that you may use and learn from all the many faces and dimensions of your life.

Allow your breath to be natural. Allow your breath to be full and quiet. Begin to feel your body, and whenever you are ready, come back and open your eyes.

WORKSHEET

Describe the mask of your hidden self. When you placed it over your face, how did it make you feel?

What was your message from anger in the west? What are your greatest fears, and how have they run your life?

Did you have feelings of abandonment in childhood? How did that affect you?

Which mask created the most change within you? Describe.

What else did you learn on your journey that shifted your perceptions of yourself?

How many masks do you think you wear in your daily life? Name them.

If you felt blocked in this exercise, describe those blocks.

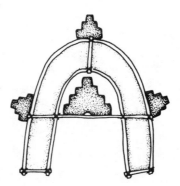

CHAPTER 6

POWER
ANIMAL
IN THE MASK

INTRODUCTION

This meditation puts you in touch with the instinctual part of your nature that is so often denied in our structured lives. This wildness that lives within you is essential to discover when you are seeking a mask of power.

EXERCISE/MEDITATION

Relax and prepare to begin a journey. Imagine in your mind's eye that you are entering a wilderness, a place of large, dark trees, smooth ground, contrasts of light and shadow. Notice that you feel safe and at home here.

Begin walking. Become aware of each footstep you take, knowing that as you walk you are coming closer to your own uniqueness, closer to true self-awareness and enlightenment. Notice that you are becoming more and more comfortable and that you are feeling strength from simply being in the Dreamtime state. Become aware of the beating of your heart, the way the gentle wind is brushing your hair. Begin to sing your power song to yourself as you walk. Feel the strength and power that it brings to your body.

You come to a clearing. You notice the light is fading as the afternoon sun begins to wane. You welcome the time when the world changes. You feel excitement, a gathered, focused readiness for this Dreamtime journey. Sit down on the ground. Feel with your whole body how your spirit is becoming tuned to the feel, the touch, even the rhythms of the earth.

Now, from out of the dark trees I, Lynn, approach you. I am holding in my hands a long sash made of bright colors—red, green, blue, yellow. It is a fertility sash. We greet each other in our spirit bodies in the Dreamtime.

I speak to you quietly, gently:

It is time for you. It is time for you to become who you are. It is time for you to become who you are by living your medicine. It is time for you to become who you are by hunting and seeking. It is time for you.

I have brought this gift of a fertility sash for you. I give it to you for one reason. You must become pregnant. You must become pregnant, not in your physical body, but in spirit. Both men and women can become pregnant with power and strength. This fertility sash that I give to you now will fill you with the power of the female, the power of the feminine that is within you. Take this colorful sash now, and tie it around your waist.

Spend some moments feeling the refinement of the fibers. Be aware of its contrasting colors. How does it feel on your body?

Notice as you tie the sash around you that you feel you are being bound, not in a negative way, but in the sense of being tightened, bound with focus, bound with power. Notice also that as you put on the sash, you smell certain herbs that have been woven into it—sage, rosemary, chamomile. The smell of the herbs mixes with the smell of the crisp air to bring you a sense of well-being; the aromas merge inside you. As you tie on your sash, you become receptive. Your power begins to be concentrated in your feminine nature, your intuition, your ability to dream, to look within the darkness, to trust. Now your womb, your center, that receptive power place in both men and women, becomes fertile for hunting. You become ready. Your womb becomes a proper receptacle for your prey. Your prey could be described as something you need in life. With your sash on, within your fertile body, you will go hunting for a special bird's egg, a winter bird's egg. I will smudge you now in the Dreamtime, cleanse you with sage and sweetgrass, so that you will be protected and ready for your journey.

Feel the flutter of an eagle feather near your face and body as I begin to smudge you with the smoke of sage that I have just lit. See with your bright eyes the abalone shell that holds the sage. Notice above us that the sky is darkening and a new moon is visible. Feel your body down to the bottoms of your feet, trusting your connection to the earth.

Now I will point you in a direction. We hug each other as a way of parting, and you begin walking. Remember to focus your energy on the area below your navel and to concentrate. Be there. Be aware of the sky, the earth, the darkness, the light. As you begin walking through the trees, feel how the trees shelter you. The air feels warmer than in the clearing where the wind was. You feel so much energy that you begin to run at a gentle pace. You cross a river and the water splashes up on your legs. The river stones feel slippery, yet you retain your balance. On the other side of the river, you come to another clearing. The moon is above you now so the light is better.

In the light of the moon you see an altar. You stop with respect. It is an altar made of stone slabs. Two thick granite slabs support a horizontal stone slab. You realize that this is a power place, a place of importance. Before going up to the altar, you take a few moments in silence to pray to the Great Spirit.

Pray to the east, asking that things of beauty and illumination be brought to you. Listen to what these things might be in the answers that the silence carries.

Pray to the south, asking that things of beauty from the south be brought to you now.

Pray to the west, asking that things of beauty from the west be brought to you now.

Pray to the north, asking that things of beauty from the north be brought to you now.

Pray to Mother Earth and Father Sky, asking that things of beauty be brought to you now. Listen in the silence for any answers or insights as to what these things of beauty may be. Trust that things of beauty from all directions are being pulled in toward you right now, whether you receive answers or not.

Now go up to the stone altar. Circle the altar four times, paying attention to your breath as you do so. Notice that your breath is regular, yet it seems so powerful, so strong, so full of intent. As you

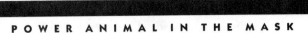

circle the altar, you notice that the altar is full of many things. There are medicine bags, beaded rattles, incense whose smoke billows out into the night, prayer sticks, many sparkling crystals, feathers, braids of sweetgrass, lit candles. You feast your eyes on this bright array of objects, offerings, food, tools. Then your eyes open wide, for now you see why you have come to this place, the power place, this place of prayer. You see, for the first time, a mask. It is a mask of your power bird or animal. It is made of fur or feathers. You wonder whether you should touch it, and then you realize you must, that this is your power and you must face your own power, become your own power, live your own power, or else you will forever be waiting for someone else to fill you with power or waiting for someone else's power to fill and fulfill you.

You take the power animal mask into your hands with reverence. You examine it, smell it. As you do so, you hear the sound of thunder in the night sky. You smile at the synchronicity. You are beginning to trust your own power. You give thanks to the Great Spirit as you place the mask over your face. The mask fits very well. It is comfortable and snug. Fur or feathers have been cut away to allow some design, and there are holes around the eyes and mouth.

When you put the mask on, you suddenly see that you are a predatory hunter, that you have always been hunting, that you are hunting for balance, for enlightenment, for truth. You are hunting to find and fulfill your own uniqueness.

A vision of me, Lynn, appears in your mind's eye now, as you begin to feel like your power animal or bird. Your body begins to move and shift as if it is coming into its true way of being, stripped of societal masks and ego facades, resting now in its own true power. You see me, and I say to you:

Feel your strength. Acknowledge your feelings, your trust in who you are. You are you, unique in all the world. Rejoice. You are going hunting. You will find the egg of the winter bird. The egg symbolizes the birth that is happening right now for you. You are giving birth to your own wholeness. Go down the ravine where the winter bird lives and find its egg. The winter bird will gladly help you in your quest if you can find its nest. The winter bird is special, for it is of the winter, when things are dark and cold, when storms rage, when we must hold to our own uniqueness and rest in the knowing that spring will come again.

The vision fades, and you are on your own to begin your journey toward the winter bird's home. You move stealthily, stalking as your power animal. You revel in the sense of action, the trust in your animalistic movements. You feel rain in the air. The whole Dreamtime world pulses with the energy of your newfound animal spirit.

You come to a place where again the woods clear and there is a large ravine, a channel of granite stones, large boulders. You realize that the stones that formed the altar came from this place. You realize also that the creek that you crossed earlier had once, long ago, crossed here. You can see the waterline on the granite walls, left by the river thousands of years ago. You wonder how the river changed, and then you realize that all things change according to their needs and some according to their power.

You sense the direction of the winter bird's nest. You are aware that there is so much more to you than you had realized. So much has been untapped but is ready now to be put to use, just as, in putting on the mask of your power animal, you have increased your ability to move with stealth.

With your power animal sense of self and your fertility sash giving you full force of being, you begin to climb the large granite boulders. Feel the touch of stone as you grasp the crevices and find strong grips to continue your quest up the side of the rock. Your mind is alert, your senses awake; the night air fills you with well-being. In a few minutes you come to a flat area, an area where dirt has settled. You wonder if the river once ran this high, ages ago. Above you and to your left you spy the nest. You climb again, and as you move slowly, you begin to pray, to sing silently a song of power for yourself, a song also of thanksgiving for the winter bird that offers its egg, its offspring to you. Take a few minutes in silence to see yourself climbing and to pray. You see the winter bird as she swoops in circles above and helps to guide you.

Now you reach the nest. With a final prayer of thanks, gently pick up the egg and secure it carefully in the pouch that is in the middle of your fertility sash. Climb back down to the flat, dirt area on the boulder. Now your breath will be your guide. You feel strong as you touch your egg, your wholeness, your food for the journeys ahead. Yet you feel inexplicably and suddenly uneasy, as if there is something else you must do. You realize that somewhere nearby is the home of your power animal, either a nest or a den. If your animal happens to be of the sea, then you must find a pond or other power place here on land where the spirit of your sea creature can touch

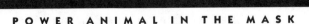

ground. Smell with your nose, feel with your hands, sense with all your senses, and move in the direction of your power animal's nest or den or pond. You can tell that your power animal lives close by. The night feels like your twin now, you feel so at home in it.

You travel a short distance across the boulders and come to a place where your power animal or bird lives. In the Dreamtime you let out a hoot, a shriek of joy, the call of your power animal. Your body feels as if it has come home. You enter the den or fly up to the nest. As you do, you see that the den or nest is filled with crystals, throwing out beautiful rainbow prisms of light. In this moment you realize that your whole life is filled with crystals if only you will believe it.

Take a moment in silence to give thanks—thanks for the knowledge of your power animal self, thanks for the egg, for wisdom and courage, for the complete circle of truth that you are discovering and will continue to discover.

Now take one crystal from the nest or den, and as you do so you feel yourself fully become your power medicine animal. You grow fur or wings, talons, claws, whiskers, paws. You are who you are in spirit, in the Dreamtime, in your animal being. Take a few moments and visualize yourself in your mind's eye walking fully as your power animal. Give thanks as you hold the crystal in your talon or paw.

When you truly feel yourself as the power animal, say to yourself, "I believe. I am. I trust." See yourself, your power animal self, lying down in the den or around the nest, and, still holding the crystal, allow yourself to fall asleep.

WORKSHEET

How did you feel when you first put on the mask of your power animal?

How did you feel when you became that animal completely? What colors did you see?

How did the power animal mask affect your feelings of personal power?

Did you feel encouraged by your power animal? In what ways?

CHAPTER 7

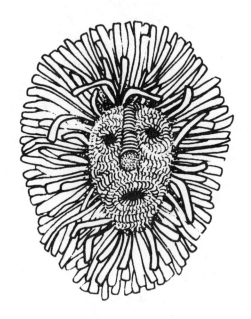

SACRED FIRE

INVOCATION OF THE FIRE SPIRITS

Spirit of the winged ones,
Great Eagle Mother,
Fly into my body,
Fly into the bodies of us all,
And bring to me,
Bring to us all,
The flaming power of the sun.

Power of the salamanders,
Awaken now!
Quicken my blood,
Quicken the blood of us all.
Power of the sun,
Carrier of my star shield,
Power of the inner fire,
Arousal of the inner flame,
Center within our spirits: Now!

INTRODUCTION

In this ceremony you will bless your shaman mask in the sacred fire that burns within your heart. You will make a commitment to your own truth. You will join with others for a stronger bond, a more powerful trusting, by becoming a part of a greater vision of peace and by being filled with the joy of community, of kinship.

EXERCISE/MEDITATION

Relax and allow your breath to be soft and gentle. Allow yourself to release any cares or worries you may have at this time. Just say silently to yourself, "I let them go." As you begin to relax, focus on your breathing. Your breath will drop down into your belly. Let your breath be like light. Let your breath fill your body with light. Imagine yourself as a beam of light. Allow yourself to move any time you feel discomfort or pain, noticing where the discomfort lies and shifting, moving always in the direction of greater comfort and joy, as we relax and breathe and begin our journey together.

Now place your consciousness on your toes and your feet. Let your feet feel strong yet relaxed, gentle yet sure of their connection to the earth. Allow your feet to feel grounded. Relax your ankles.

Relax your lower legs and your calves, allowing your breath to be natural and full. Relax your knees and the backs of your knees. Let your thighs rest, and let your sexual center and your buttocks relax. Let your belly be at peace. Do not hold any tension or fear or worry in your midsection. Imagine that your stomach and the organs of your midsection are relaxing, doing their work gently, easily, peacefully. Relax now your chest, your ribs. Your heart and lungs relax so that your breath and your pulse are slow and wonderful. Take a moment to give thanks for your breath, for the air that you breathe, for the pathway of light that you walk on, which is your journey of life. Relax your shoulders, letting all the cares and worries that you hold on your shoulders just drop away gently. Relax your shoulders and your arms and your hands. Check to see that your hands are relaxed. So much changes when we relax ourselves. Relax especially your hands so that you are not gripping too tightly to this world, so that you are not gripping too tightly to your problems. Learn to let go. Relax your neck, shifting it if necessary. Allow your jaw to drop, your facial muscles to relax. Relax your scalp and let your eyes relax and the muscles behind your eyes so that soon your whole body is relaxed, peaceful, centered.

Now in your mind's eye, in your imagination, with spirit, in your own way, we are going to take a journey. There is a place in California where you can see two mountains, two sacred mountains, two huge and powerful mountains. We are going to take a journey in order to perform a ceremony with the sacred fire and your masks of power in a place where we can see these two powerful mountains. These mountains are Mount Shasta and Mount Lassen. It does not matter if you have never actually seen these mountains. Imagine them huge and powerful and snowcapped, like two points of strong energy in the world, because today our journey is a joining of the energy of two strong points. Today we are going to sit with Agnes Whistling Elk around the sacred fire.

We live in a new time, as all times are new times. We live in a time of change and of power. We live in a time of fear and ignorance. We live in a time where we must call more strength and joy into our lives, into the lives of those around us, and most especially into the life of the earth. For this we will join together around the sacred fire, because there is power and strength and peace in joining together.

Imagine yourself walking through a dense forest, along a stream, hearing the sound of the stream. Birds chirp near the water. Carrying your shaman mask of power, you walk slowly, casually, leisurely, yet as you walk, you are focused on your commitment to yourself and to your lifework. As you walk, you realize that you are committed to seeking enlightenment. As you walk, you realize that there are helpers and friends along the path. As you walk, you feel joy in your heart, because you know that you will soon join a circle of friends and guides and teachers. Everyone will walk to the mountain in his or her own way, and it will be as if you are walking alone. There is no one with you in the forest near the stream, but as you walk, you are aware that there will be other people who will join you on top of the mountain, the mountain that has no name, the mountain from which you can see both Mount Shasta and Mount Lassen, two points of power in this state of California.

Now find a place along the path to sit, to rest quietly, and take a few moments in silence to say a prayer—a prayer for yourself, a prayer for your life, a prayer that will give you strength for your journey.

After you have said your prayer, continue walking and let your breath be gentle, natural. As you walk through the forest, along the stream, begin to pay attention. Begin to look for something, some object that you will find on the path that will represent your commitment to your own truth. It may be anything. It may be a stone, a twig, a leaf—something that symbolizes your commitment, your responsibility, your willingness to follow your own path of heart.

As you walk, you are paying attention to each foot as it falls on the earth, placing one foot after the other, taking things one step at a time. Walk as the mouse walks, as the small creatures walk, in trust and innocence, looking only at what is before you yet feeling confident, sure of your journey and your destination. Your eyes are bright, filled with the beauty of the forest. Your heart beats gently. Your mind is at rest as your feet touch the earth. You find your object and hold it in your hands, and as you walk toward the mountain, through the forest, near the stream, you think about your object and what it represents; you know, deep inside, that it represents your commitment, your trust, your willingness to participate and join with others. We are entering a time when we are each responsible for others. So many of us have been on a journey that we consider our own individual path. Now is the time when all individuals must join in groups and clans, in families, in communities. We must join together in order to build the energy we need for the work of the earth, the work that we must do. This work is calling us now. Let yourself take a moment in silence as you walk through the forest, feeling the wind blow through the trees, taking a moment in silence to think about the necessity of healing this earth.

Soon you come to a clearing in the forest. It is near the base of the mountain. You look up at the mountain, and you do not see anyone. While you are standing at the bottom of the mountain, you are alone. But offering a prayer of thanks and again focusing on trust and innocence and commitment to taking things one step at a time, you begin to hike up the mountain. The mountain is covered with manzanita, which is a low bush with a rich, red bark. You wind your way up the mountain on deer trails, and you give thanks for the fact of deer living in safety and beauty in these mountains.

As you walk up the mountain in silence, you begin to see other people, and you give thanks for these people. So often in our lives, we curse or condemn or bemoan the fact that others are with us or are crowding our space. Now is the time to open your heart and rejoice that there are others with you, that there are others of like mind, of like kind, who will share in the process of helping heal the earth, helping each other heal ourselves. As you hike up the mountain, take time to stop and rest and sit, looking out. You can see parts of one mountain, Shasta or Lassen, depending on where you are in your hike. You realize that you will soon be able to see the two points of power at one time, and you know that there you will be on your own point of power, that together we will form a circle of power, a circle of love, a circle of joy, a circle of growth. So take time to rest as you go up the path. So many of us are working so hard, yet often we are doing so only because we feel we are so far behind. From this moment forward, you will never be behind. You will always be within the circle that you are about to join. So rest; take time; rest and take time.

As you continue walking, enjoy the movement. Imagine your breath being taxed, and give thanks for this. Give thanks for the work and the effort it takes to climb a mountain. Soon you reach the top. It is a wide area. It is almost as if God or the Great Spirit— whatever name we use for the powers that be—has purposely made this mountain wide at the top, rather than coming to a point. And you realize that this is a perfect place for the circle to form. This is the perfect place for the first meeting around the sacred fire in the Dreamtime. Soon, many people are there. You naturally form a circle, sitting on the top of the mountain. Everyone is looking around and smiling, and somehow you all know to keep silence. You all begin to hold hands.

Then I, Lynn, stand and walk into the middle of the circle. I tell you this:

We look in all directions and we see. We are at the top of the mountain, and we can see Mount Lassen, place of power, and Mount Shasta, place of power and light. We call in the energy of these sacred mountains to be with us now. We call in the energy of all the living things as far as we can see—the spirit of plants and animals, the wind and rocks—to be with us now. I call in the spirit of the forty-four sisters of the Sisterhood of the Shields. Sacred teachers, I know you are watching us and guiding us and approving and are glad today that these people are here. Now, I ask Agnes Whistling Elk to appear before us—she of the ancient world, she of the modern world, she of the Dreamtime, she of the time of day and night. Agnes, my teacher, my friend, come and be with us now.

Soon we see Agnes appear from the south of the circle, and she walks around the outside of the circle and enters through the east door, carrying her mask of power. Feel your heart lift as you see this ancient Indian woman with two long braids of dark gray hair. Her face is lined and furrowed, yet she walks and even looks young, for she has a youthful vibrancy. Agnes stands in the middle of the circle with me, and this is what she says:

I am Agnes Whistling Elk, and my heart is full to be here with you. I welcome you into my circle. I know that sometimes fear is mixed with your love. You have felt doubt of your own truth, and you have felt anger through-out your whole life. You have tried to push this doubt and this anger away. That is all right, but now I ask you to let your doubt and your anger rise, because you must drop deeper, and doubt and anger can be your teachers. When you are doubting or angry, drop deeper inside yourself to a new place of personal truth.

Many of you have waited a long time to see me. Many of you have confusion about where I have been. Each of us has our own path, and my path is the path of sisterhood and mystery. My path is the path of joy. My path is the path of many masks. My path is the path of the invisible truth and deep trust. Those of you who are doing this meditation are here because you have that deep trust. You have that faith in yourself and in the power of the world, the power of Mother Earth, the power of believing in nothing but the life force and the light. Join hands, if you are with a partner or friends; join hands lightly yet firmly; join hands and be silent.

I will now dig a small pit, a fire pit, here in the center of our circle. The fire represents the warmth, the creation of light, the creation of healing power. We will bless the shaman masks that you carry. We will pray in silence now and feel the energy move through the circle. Feel the warmth of hands touching each other, as I dig this fire pit and welcome you to the sacred fire, the fire that I will build. I thank you for being here and for trusting that we do this work together. Though I cannot be with all of you in your daily lives face to face, I am with you in spirit. I am with you in the Dreamtime. Thus, I am with you truly in your daily life. This you must trust, for it is in trust that we find movement. When we do not trust, we become mired in procrastination, in stagnation, in death.

Today we are to join together for a stronger bond, a more powerful trusting. I have dug the pit. I have built the fire. Now I gather the sticks and kindling for the fire. I give thanks to this place in the earth for allowing us to make a fire here, for offering this place of power. And with these wooden matches, we start the fire.

Great Spirit, Mother Earth,
All the powers and all the directions,
To my teachers who are everywhere,
I give thanks and prayer.
And I call these people together to be with us.
May the people remember their sacred beings,
That the Great Spirit lives within each of us.

Now Lynn and I will sit by the fire holding our shaman masks, and Lynn will pass wood to feed the fire as necessary. Each person here, holding your shaman face, will come and sit beside us one at a time. When we embrace, feel the power; feel the joy, because I want you to use this embracing over and over again in your life as a way of centering, of making contact with me and with the sacred fire that burns within each of our hearts.

We call upon the powers of the two great mountains, Shasta and Lassen, to help us and guide us. Each of you, starting in the east, come, one at a time, and I will give you a message. This is my message to you for your work, for your heart, for your being with us. Work with this message; understand this message; be filled with this message. You and I are together, and all of us are together. Lynn is my sister, my daughter, my great mes-

senger who walks the paths of the world, while I walk the path behind the world and within the world.

Now that Agnes has finished speaking, I want you, in your own time and your own way, to imagine yourself getting up. You meet with Agnes, showing your mask to her and to the fire, and you embrace near the fire. Then Agnes tells you to pass your mask gently over the fire, and you feel the warmth of the flames, and you know that this warmth symbolizes the light and the love and the warmth of the sacred fire. You take your stick or your stone or your leaf, whatever you found on the path, and you put it on the other side of the fire. You make a statement about your commitment to your own truth. This is done spontaneously; there is no need to think. Let this statement come from your heart and your soul, from your spirit and your joy in life. After you have placed your object and spoken your commitment to living your medicine, listen in silence while Agnes gives you her message. Listen and remember, and embrace Agnes again. Then put on your mask, knowing that it is blessed, and return to your place in the circle.

In silence and in remembrance, you watch as others, one by one, join their truth and masks with yours over the sacred fire. Keep silence, as you all become part of a greater vision of peace. You remember and learn from Agnes directly—remember her feeling, her love, and her embrace, and remember her teaching and her message for you. And as you sit in silence, observe the other powerful shaman masks, each one unique with its feathers, symbols, and brilliant colors. Watch the stones and the twigs, the leaves, the feathers—any objects that you and the others found along the path to represent your commitment—watch them grow into a sculpture, a spontaneous sculpture that we will leave here. So sit now in silence as you remember.

In time we are all together. You have all embraced Agnes in the center. Now hold hands around the fire. Agnes again speaks, and this is what she says:

There are many paths. There are many ways to go. There are many truths. There are many falsehoods. This path that you have chosen, this circle that you have chosen, this life that you have chosen—let it be filled with joy; let it be filled with wisdom. We are working together. We are honoring each other, and I honor you on your sacred path. You are greater than you imagine, yet let yourself be humble. Let us join together around this circle of power. Let us feel the warmth of our embrace, of our hands touching, of our sacred fire. Let us help heal this earth, and make the changes necessary for health and wisdom and beauty. Ho.

When Agnes has finished speaking, no one says a word, but everyone looks and feels different. You can feel the pulse in each other's hands. Then, spontaneously, everyone releases hands. In your own way, say a silent prayer, asking for strength and guidance and wisdom to journey back down the mountain. Each of us, when we journey alone, needs the strength and love of the others. It is easy to feel powerful on top of the mountain. Know that you can call on this mountain of strength when you feel alone, because from this point forward you shall never be truly alone. The Great Spirit is part of you. Your shaman face is part of you. Take the message that Agnes has given you and work with it. Dream with it. Be with it. Trust it. Let it work in your life. Be strong. Let your gifts to the sacred fire be strong. Let your heart be open as you go now down the mountain. Let yourself always remember this place of power between two sacred mountains. Walk gently. Walk peacefully. Walk in balance and beauty.

Soon you find yourself alone in the forest again, yet you do not feel alone. You feel filled with love, with the loving embrace of Agnes, the loving touch of the members of our circle. You feel filled with the joy of community, of kinship.

Now you begin to feel your body, and the forest fades. Your body feels strong. You feel your feet and your legs, your arms and hands. You give thanks for your body as you begin to focus on your breath, and you allow yourself to move and release any tension. In your own way, at your own time, when you are ready, you may open your eyes, fully conscious, fully relaxed, fully in your body. We are together in spirit, in body, in mind, in heart. We are together as a circle. And you are in the room with your eyes open, wide awake.

WORKSHEET

How did you feel when you saw Agnes Whistling Elk?

What message did Agnes have for you? How will you use her message in your life?

What objects did you find along your path to represent your commitment?

Describe the sacred fire. How did you feel when you looked around the sacred fire and saw all the masks of power?

How did your mask feel after it had been blessed by the sacred fire?

Did the sacred fire change your feelings about life? Explain.

CHAPTER 8

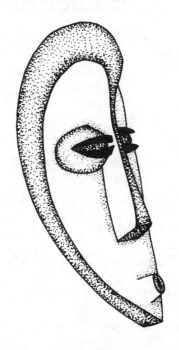

THE AROUSAL
OF THE
INNER FIRE

INTRODUCTION

There are different ways to talk about the "arousal of the inner fire." There is an ancient science that comes to us from the East, called raising the kundalini, or serpent power. The kundalini is a primal energy that begins in the root chakra. It is pictured as a coiled serpent that lives always within your being until you evolve and clear yourself to the degree that the serpent can be awakened. There are many ways to do this. The "arousal of the inner fire" is what I might call a relative of raising the kundalini. It is not the same process exactly. Raising the kundalini can be a very dangerous process, because the kundalini energy, as it moves up on two different paths through the chakra system, creates tremendous heat and can actually burn the myelin sheaths around the nerves. Certainly when you have raised the kundalini, you are left with much greater perception, sometimes enlightenment, certainly much higher and greater gifts than when you began. For this reason, some people strive for many lifetimes to awaken the coiled serpent.

Another related process is that of self-immolation. History includes many stories of great saints, masters, medicine men and women who choose to die by self-immolation. They burn from the inside out, and when the burning is complete, not an ash is left. This occurs, as I have been taught, because when you self-immolate, you can take your physical form into the nagual—that is, to the other side, to the spirit side, where you can also perform other special acts, where you progress into different aspects of power. If you self-immolate, supposedly you can take your body back from the spirit world and manifest it in its physical form at will. The process gives you the ability to move between the dimensions and to take physical form, if you wish.

The "arousal of the inner fire" is a process that was taught to me by the Sisterhood of the Shields, and it has to do with awakening your ability to move into past lives. The "arousal of the inner fire" can be experienced as a quickening in the blood, because your karma and your past lives are held within the blood. Interestingly enough, you do not necessarily come to the inner fire through heightened physical activity, although that is one path. The way that I am going to teach you is quite different. It is through your own silence, your emptiness, that you find the source of creation. The source of creation is heat and, therefore, fire. But to find that fire, you must first find the ultimate sense of self, the ultimate sense of your own being.

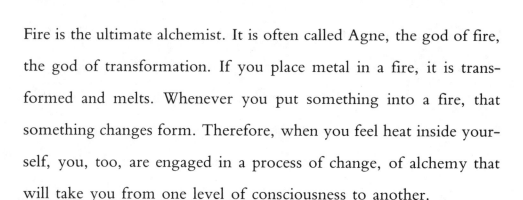

Fire is the ultimate alchemist. It is often called Agne, the god of fire, the god of transformation. If you place metal in a fire, it is transformed and melts. Whenever you put something into a fire, that something changes form. Therefore, when you feel heat inside yourself, you, too, are engaged in a process of change, of alchemy that will take you from one level of consciousness to another.

EXERCISE/MEDITATION

Take a deep breath. Let all of your thoughts pass from your mind. Totally and completely relax all of your muscles from the tips of your toes up through the trunk of your body.

Take another deep breath, as you feel the energy of Mother Earth spiraling up your spine. Relax all of the tiny muscles along your backbone and between your shoulder blades and in your shoulders. Pull the energy up through your throat. Swallow once hard. Then relax all the muscles in your face—around your mouth, your eyes, your ears, in your forehead, and in your scalp.

Now feel yourself being surrounded by the golden white light of the Divine Mother, the white light of creation. On the outside of that white light, visualize green light—the color of heart and love and the nature spirits.

As you let all of the old images fade from your mind, I would like you to imagine that you are walking in a meadow. It is beautifully green. It is springtime, or perhaps early summer. You are in a place of wilderness, serenity, and beauty. There is no one for miles and miles around, and you feel the warm air on your skin. You hear the birds in the trees. Flowers are blooming in the meadow—red, blue, white, and yellow. Off in the distance, you hear the sound of rushing water. You are drawn to that sound. It comes from a mountain that is sloping down into the meadow, and you walk toward it. As you get closer, the sound grows louder, and you see in the distance a waterfall, shimmering silver in the sunlight. You walk over to the stream. When you finally come to it, you dip your fingers in the rushing water. It is icy cold, and you know that it has come from the height of the mountains above. You look up to the mountains, and you see the white peaks silhouetted against the blue sky. You feel great power from the mountains and a kinship with their stillness and serenity.

You walk downstream and there you notice a large, flat stone in the middle of the stream; the water rushes by on both sides and goes on its way. You know that this stone is what Agnes Whistling Elk has described as a "sleeping stone." It is large and flat, as large as you are tall, and looks like an altar in the center of the stream. A sleeping stone is a stone altar meant for dreaming. It is often the center of a world, meaning that it has been endowed with energy and power from higher beings. It is meant for people of all faiths and all beliefs. It assists you in your dreaming and in your initiations. You recognize this stone and yearn to touch it and to sit upon it.

It is a warm, sunny day, and there is no one around for miles. You decide to strip off your clothes and walk out through the stream and sit on the sleeping stone. As you enter the water, you find that it is icy cold, and you move quickly. You pull yourself up onto the stone. It is easily big enough for you to lie down on. You do so until your body is warm again from the sun. Then a voice inside you tells you to sit up on the stone and look downstream. The voice inside tells you, as you watch the rushing water moving away from you, that you are facing your past—that the water rushing ahead of you is like all of the debris, all of the joy, all of the sorrow, everything, your baggage that you have collected throughout your many life-times. It is rushing by and disappearing around the bend.

I would like you to take a few moments to sit there in your Dreamtime and contemplate the past that is rushing away and to realize that your future is behind you, coming toward you, but you cannot see it. You can only see the past, rushing by. Think to your-self, as you contemplate the movement of the past, what you would like to throw into the river and be rid of forever.

Take some time.

Now take a deep breath, remembering what you threw away into the river, and carefully turn around on the sleeping stone. With reverence, face your future, face the water that is coming down from the waterfall and surging toward you. Contemplate what that looks like to you, what it means to you, realizing now that you have your back to your past and you are facing what is new and fresh. What is it that you would like to have come to you in the future? What is it that you have asked for? What seeds have you sown so that the fruits that ripen on your tree will be sweet? Take some time, and contem-

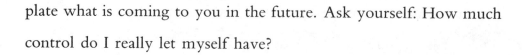

plate what is coming to you in the future. Ask yourself: How much
control do I really let myself have?

Now you have spent much time contemplating your past and
your future, and you are getting sleepy. The sun is very warm and
feels wonderful on your body, and you decide to lie down on the
sleeping stone. The sleeping stone enables you to dream, and as you
close your eyes, you move into a very deep trance, taking several
deep breaths, allowing your body to relax, feeling the warmth of the
sun on your skin, relaxing all of your muscles completely. You are
still conscious of the sound of the water rushing by. It rushes by you
on your left and on your right, leaving you very centered. You move
your consciousness into your shaman center, sensing the power and
the energy of the water force around you. It reminds you of the
power and strength of the life force of the universe. You are, indeed,
centered within the cycles of pandemonium we call life. Slowly, you
find a sense of stillness with the water rushing around you, just as
everyday life surges around you like a whirlwind. As you breathe
deeply, you realize that those whirlpools of energy can swirl endlessly around you and you need not move. You need not stir your

being. You are like the center of a cyclone, living in a place of stillness and quiet and ever-present power.

You find yourself dreaming of being a cloud, floating in the sky, supported by the hand of the Great Mother, much as a bird is supported by the air in flight. You see yourself floating endlessly and quietly on the flowing power of eternity. You need do nothing. There is no effort that needs to be made. You need only to be, as you float in the stillness, in the quiet, in the center of your own universe. As you experience yourself as the still point, at the center, you realize that you are surrounded by golden white light that looks and feels almost like cotton, like angel hair. It is like a cocoon that has softly formed around you to protect you. It cradles you as you float. You feel safe and powerful and at ease, completely and totally at ease. Take several minutes just to float in endless peace and joy.

You realize that you could stay in this floating domain of selfhood and quiet forever. You would be complete. There is nothing more that you would need to do. Inside this place of stillness is the source of creation. Inside this place of stillness lives all that you truly are. It is the home of your sacred witness, who watches and absorbs all of reality. If there is not stillness, there is no true understanding of reality, because to understand reality is to understand the stillness, the source of creation.

The source of creation has many faces. Like all things, it is positive and negative. Like all things, it is hot and cold. The heat is the inner fire. Arousing the inner fire requires first that you find this place of stillness. Now that you have found it, even if you have only experienced it for a moment, you have done what you need to do. To find your way back, you simply retrace the steps that you have just covered.

As you lie in the silence, surrounded in golden light, take your mind slowly back to the river and the sleeping stone. Remember the experience of sitting on the stone and looking downstream at your past rushing by and then turning to watch the stream and your future surging toward you, like all of the power of creation.

Take a deep breath and go still deeper, into the interior of your body. Imagine your blood system, the veins of your body, like tributaries of a stream, the main arteries, your heart, the main rivers of your body, the rivers of life and life force that move throughout your tissues. See the prime mover and motivator of your blood flow, your heart. I would like you now to move your consciousness up into your heart. Take several minutes to look around inside your heart, feeling all around you the green light that emanates from that chakra, feeling how this light expands your heart chakra. Feel the love that emanates from your heart. Explore inside, seeing, perhaps, the form of your fears and the form of your loves.

Take a deep breath, and let those images fade away.

Now look around inside your heart. Find the center of your heart, the seat of power, and find a room, a magnificent room, like a throne room. Use your imagination. Imagine its grandeur. You find in the center of this room an altar. It is spread with sacred icons, bundles, items of all kinds that relate to you. You sit on a blanket in front of the altar. As you sit there, it is important that you stay in touch with your shaman center, that area around your navel where your shaman will lives. Take a moment to sit before your altar, the altar of your heart, and feel your heart opening to the universe, to the light, to the wonder of your body. Realize that your heart creates an incredible source of power within you. Your heart beats every day

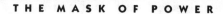

and every night for your entire life without you even being conscious of it most of the time. I would like you to give thanks to your heart, and for a few moments, take time to feel the power of the entity known as your heart, pulling the energy up from your solar plexus. Your heart is like a clearinghouse for your emotions. See them moving through. Do not hold onto any of them, but watch them as they come through. Just simply witness, as you sit at your altar. Let yourself feel anything that comes up, and witness as it comes and goes, like a flowing river.

Take a moment.

It is now time for you to experience a quickening. A quickening is felt when you observe your first past life within your own blood system. As you look around the inside of your heart, you will see that veins come in and out. There are arteries that move in and out of your heart, and I want you to move down one of those larger arteries, realizing that as you move through these arteries, you are actually moving into the very fluid of your life force. The color of your blood is a magnificent red. It is the color of Mother Earth, the

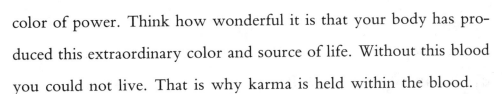

color of power. Think how wonderful it is that your body has produced this extraordinary color and source of life. Without this blood you could not live. That is why karma is held within the blood.

Just as you found the sleeping stone in the center of the stream, you now find the "seat of the jaguar" sitting above the bloodstream in the middle of the artery. You move toward that seat and sit upon it, looking downstream. The seat of the jaguar is magnificently carved. The arms of the chair are the heads of jaguars. The seat fits you perfectly; it was made for you. Traditionally, this is the seat of power for the shaman. It is the seat of perfect vision of the past, future, and present. It is the seat of the jaguar, the seat of forgetting and remembering. It is the place of nonaddiction and no fear. It is the place of taking our power. To be true shamans, we must know of our past lives and of our future lives. To experience this quickening, you must move deeply into the feeling of the blood rushing around you on either side.

As you sit in the place of the jaguar, close your eyes and be conscious of your shaman center. I would like you to take in seven short breaths, and then breathe out seven short breaths, tensing your solar plexus, and again breathe in seven short breaths and breathe out

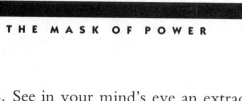

seven short breaths. See in your mind's eye an extraordinary fire, a bonfire. See it flaming in front of you. Watch the flames as they dance in the night sky. Feel the intensity of their heat, hear the sound of the crackling fire. Feel the heat of that fire in your root chakra. See the colors—flames of orange, red, bright gold, and yellow. Feel the flames all around you. Watch that fire dancing, drawing ever-changing designs in the night sky. As you watch those flames, you begin to feel as if you, too, are dancing. You actually imagine that you are becoming one of those flames. Feel your power and your heat and your strength and your ability to burn anything in your path. Feel that sense of inner fire and power around your shaman will, at first feeling it just inside you, and then beginning to extend it around you a foot or two, realizing that you are the source of that fire. Then see it extending four or five feet. You are a huge fire burning, and you are in total control of that fire. Then slowly bring those flames down and back to about a foot around you. Now see the fire moving back inside you, inside your shaman center, giving you extraordinary healing abilities, extraordinary strength.

Fire is sacred. It is the transformer, the alchemist of nature. The fire of the sun is our great source of light and life. Without the sun, nothing could live. You have a sun within you. You have that fire waiting to be ignited. Ignite it now, and let it burn, as you sit on the seat of the jaguar.

Move your consciousness into deep trance. Take another deep breath, and move even more deeply into your source. Begin to hear the sound of the blood rushing by, like the rushing river that you have so often heard. It is a magnificently beautiful sight, like a magnificent sunset, red, purple, pink, and orange, turning to flowing water and surrounding you with power.

As you sit looking downstream, you begin to move back in time. Slowly move back, perhaps fifty years, and see how that feels to you as you look at the surge of the river moving past you. Then move back, perhaps a hundred or two hundred years, back into history. Let your mind wander. Let your heart expand, and bring the energy up constantly from your shaman center, letting your heart be full of love, remembrance, and wisdom. And in the passing blood, see your lives before you. If one feels right to you, if it feels like you want to move into that experience, simply do so. Move your consciousness out of the jaguar seat, out of your veins and into that time frame. Just let your mind go. Do not doubt. Do not judge. Simply trust that what is happening is part of the sacred Dreamtime, that you are, indeed, in the center of a quickening. Just let it happen; let it flow. Simply move back in time to whatever is in store for you. I will give you several minutes. Be sure to take something from the lifetime you experience—a ring, a piece of material, a stone, a crystal, or whatever—so you can put it on the altar of your heart when you come back. Journey safely.

Take some time.

Take a deep breath and come carefully out of this lifetime that you have found. Let the images fade very slowly. Take whatever it is that you have found, a stone or a crystal, a piece of jewelry—take it with you, knowing that you have experienced something very profound. Have respect for what you have experienced. Feel yourself sitting on the seat of the jaguar.

Take another deep breath, and then turn, step out of the jaguar seat, and move back into the room within your heart. Sit before your altar and light two candles, two white candles. Bless yourself with sage, and then place whatever you have brought back from this past life on the altar. Thank the Great Spirit, the powers of the four directions, the Great Mother, your medicine and power animals, and your guardians for allowing you to have this experience. Now think to yourself, "What have I learned from what I have just experienced? How did this past life enlighten me? How does it relate to my current life? What understanding has this past life given me that will help me in my current one?"

Take a few moments.

Now take another deep breath, and with gratitude for your heart and the source of power that your heart is, move your consciousness out of your body, up through the top of your head, and become aware again of your entire body. Become aware of the room. Move your toes and your fingers, feeling the energy of Mother Earth washing down over your face, down over your shoulders and your arms, down over the trunk of your body, down into your legs, and spiraling back up your spine and back into your system. When it feels comfortable to do so, open your eyes.

WORKSHEET

Write down what you found on your journey. What did you bring back from that lifetime? What lessons do you feel that you have learned?

How did this past life enlighten you? How does it relate to your life

this time around?

Describe the wilderness place to which you traveled in this visualization. How did it affect you?

What from the past did you throw away into the river? What did you ask to come to you in the future?

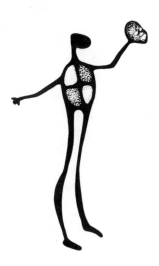

What did it feel like to sit in the seat of the jaguar? What was your impression of this place of power?

PRAYER OF THANKSGIVING

Great Spirit,
I honor you all the waking days of my life.
O great wise ones,
Who guide us on our sacred journey,
You know when to reveal the mysteries of truth,
Just as the clouds part
And allow us to see the snowcapped mountains
That were obscured from view.

I am learning that truth burns like a fire,
And when I am filled with psychic debris
That I have collected in my experiences
Through my lifetime,
Truth, at the wrong moment,
Can burn me beyond recognition.

Thank you, Great Spirit,
For helping me understand
That my journey is a careful one
And that I must place each foot carefully on the path,
Walking with judgment and discernment.
It is inappropriate to run wildly and carelessly
On this sacred journey.

Even with this knowledge,
I am grateful for my spontaneity
And my wildness of spirit.
I understand the difference
Between the wildness of my own soul
And carelessness and thoughtlessness
On my path to evolution.

As I look out at my sacred landscape,
I see great boulders that look like eagles

And clouds that look like wolves,
Passing above me in the sky.
The great thunderhead clouds
Reflect kachina dolls dancing
In the spirit world across the sacred plains.

The mountains rise majestically above the clouds,
And the rivers flow like luminous fibers of silver
Through the life force of my universe.
I hold hands with my sisters and my brothers,
Committed to harmony and peace
And an understanding of the human condition.

Truth has many names,
But all truth is the same.
Those who say that they know the truth,
Know nothing.
And those who say that they know nothing,
Know the truth.

Thank you, Great Spirit,
For this magnificent schoolhouse that we call earth.
Thank you, Great Spirit,
For the winged ones and the four-leggeds
And the two-leggeds.
Thank you for the plants and the trees and the stones
That were here before us and that teach us so many things.

I give you my trust, Great Spirit,
As you have given me my life.
Thank you for your blessings.
Ho!

EPILOGUE

I hope that your journey through the making of your shaman face has been a fruitful one. I want you to remember that you have delved into deep and dark recesses of your subconscious mind, and you have brought up a lot of things that may be difficult to look at or hard to face. Be kind to yourself. Allow yourself some time to adjust to the new realities you have experienced. Making a shaman face can change your life forever, for it gives you new vision; it gives you a new way of seeing.

As with all things in the world of power, a ceremony is only as powerful as the person performing it. The symbolism that you use and the tools that you have, including your shaman face, serve as a bridge from ordinary consciousness to altered and more powerful states. Remember that these tools are in need of energy, so the more you use your shaman face, the more powerful it will be. Do not close this book and then forget what you have done here. Give yourself a chance to rest, and then come back to the ideas, images, and impressions that you have written down. Come back and reflect. When you do this, you will realize that you have already grown. You have already begun to manifest your sacred dreams in the world. Give thanks to yourself for the powers that you have invoked. Acknowledge how special you are in this world. We never seem to give ourselves enough credit for what we have done. We always think that we could have done more, that even though we have had extraordinary visions and experiences, other people have had better ones, more powerful ones. But you cannot compare one person's experiences to those of another, just as you cannot compare apples and oranges. There is no other human being who is just like you. Therefore, you cannot be compared to anyone. Your experience is unique and magnificent unto yourself. It is as private or as public as you wish it to be. It is yours and it is sacred. Honor the place of beauty and strength within your own heart. Wear your shaman face in your ceremonies with power, and be proud of all that you have accomplished, for you have come a long way.

For the next four seasons of the year, let your shaman face rest on your altar or a sacred place near you. Keep it wrapped in red natural material for one year's passing, always blessing it with sage or sweetgrass before and after wearing it.

I send thanks from my heart to yours for joining me on this path of beauty.

> The answer to any question has already been written within your own silence. You need only take time to stop and listen to the heartbeat of the Great Spirit.
> — *The Power Deck*

TASK PAGE

It would be of great help to you to take the time to write a summary of your life wearing the masks, the personas, that you have always worn. Then, as if you were composing a myth, rewrite your life as it would have been had you been wearing your shaman face of power. How would your vision have been different? Would you have chosen the same people, circumstances, and career? Change the outcome of your life to one of power and magic. Meditate on the feelings that this gives you.

EPILOGUE

TASK PAGE

Write a prayer of thanks for the work you are allowing yourself
to do.

For the past ten years I have been describing my learning and my path. It has been a joy to do this. As I continue my journey, I would be grateful if you would share your insights with me.

Please write to me at the following address:

Lynn Andrews
2934 1/2 Beverly Glen Circle
Box 378
Los Angeles, CA 90077
800-726-0082

Please send your name and address so I can share any new information with you about my work.

Tapes are available for all of the meditations in this book. For information, call Lynn Andrews Productions at the number listed above.